(GRADES 4-8)

CONNECTING WISELY IN THE DIGITAL AGE

BY DEVORAH HEITNER, PH.D
AND KAREN JACOBSON, M.A.

SOCIAL/EMOTIONAL INSIGHTS & SKILLS FOR PLUGGED-IN KIDS

Published by YouthLight, Inc. | www.youthlight.com

Design by Melody Taylor
Project Editing by Susan Bowman

ISBN: 978-1-59850-172-8

Library of Congress Number: 2014958732

10 9 8 7 6 5 4 3 2 1
Printed in the United States

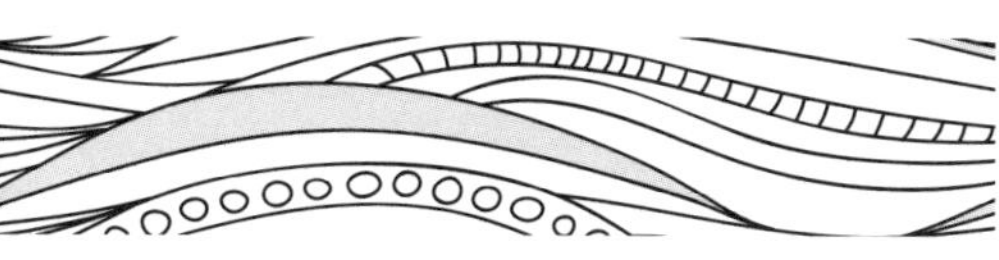

TABLE OF

CONTENTS

Introduction

Why this book?

In our work with schools and youth organizations, we regularly encounter leaders who are concerned about young people's experiences with technology. These teachers and leaders see their students distracted or stressed by interpersonal issues that are intensified and exacerbated by technology.

The tendency for young people to focus on physical appearance is made worse since they can be photographed by anyone at any time. Sharing images and "selfies" is a major part of online self-presentation, or building a "profile." Even texting, which seems quite simple to adults, can be a minefield for kids. Group texts are both annoying and somehow irresistible to new texters. Texting impatience is an annoyance many of your students will recognize.

Family relationships can be strengthened by technology, but that same technology also causes stress when parents' work challenges and young people's peer relationships follow them into the home. In addition, when children or parents are "plugged in," it takes away from family connection time. The exercises in this curriculum open up spaces for students to address these challenges, find validation and community with their experiences, and build empathy for their peers around these shared experiences.

Young people independently communicating with others their age is nothing new, but now that their communication is made more visible to adults though the digital world, what is the responsibility of schools, counselors, teachers, and parents in mentoring young people?

Social media places more everyday stress on a broad range of children. Young players encounter mean behavior in online gaming spaces that can carry over into peer relationships. They witness social events that they are excluded from, sometimes in real time through photo and video sharing. Belonging to a peer group is of vital importance for all of us, so as painful as this might be for adults, it is much more difficult for children and teenagers.

Children and teens have access to all kinds of digital devices from increasingly young ages. Many of our students, instead of wading slowly into the world of digital communication with their peers, are diving in head first, moving from a fairly unplugged social life as a young child— facilitated by parents and comprised of mostly structured activities—to having a significant peer social life through texting, social media and shared gameplay that their parents may or may not engage in or even be aware of. Young people independently communicating with others their age is nothing new, but now that their communication is made more visible to adults though the digital world, what is the responsibility of schools, counselors, teachers, and parents in mentoring young people?

These young people don't get "training wheels" in the social uses of technology. Instead, in many families, parents make all social arrangements for their children, right up until those children receive their very own phone, which suddenly brings with it the daunting responsibility of managing their own social lives. This responsibility is shifted to young people with very little preparation and practice. The exercises in this book offer that practice in dealing with everyday social issues and the way they translate into the digital realm. These lessons challenge students to think critically about how to relate with friends via texting and social media.

Young people don't get "training wheels" in the social uses of technology.

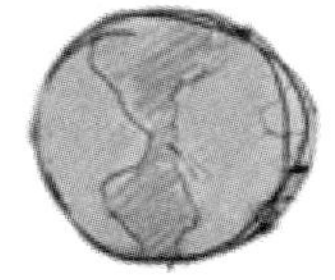

Children often begin using computers and other connected devices at a young age; many schools require laptops or provide laptops or tablets as part of the curriculum. Teachers describe classroom management challenges, like distraction, and report that online social issues affect the classroom and school community. Parents and schools need to educate children about how to use these devices in a responsible way, how to control impulses and think before acting. There are some excellent resources on internet safety, but very little has been written about mentoring students through the social emotional experiences of growing up in a highly connected world. The exercises in this curriculum are written to support the social process kids engage in as they become techno-independent, either with their own devices or through access to shared devices. This digital coming-of-age process is formative to their growing personality, their sense of self, their ethics and their position as a member of the community.

As digital citizenship educators, we have seen countless examples of children and teens making online mistakes they regret or being hurtful to others. Many schools have tried to control student behavior by emphasizing the negative legal and social consequences of poor online choices. In contrast, our curriculum emphasizes critical thinking and empathy and offers students space to reflect in their own group context.

The goal of this curriculum is to offer the students in your program ways to identify, analyze and solve common problems they will face in grades four through eight growing up with technology. This guide facilitates conversations and engagement. Unlike guides to general internet safety, this curriculum is focused on how young people shape their online communication with people they know and how their experiences affect them on a day to day basis.

One of the challenges educators, school counselors and youth mentors face is that we are teaching students in a rapidly changing media environment. In the last two years, tablet ownership for families with young children leapt from 8% to 40%, and the percentage of children with access to some sort of smart mobile device at home increased from 52% to 75% (2011, Lenhart, et.al.). In the schools we work in, large numbers of fifth graders have cellphones or smartphones, and by seventh grade phones are universal. These children's parents, while rightly concerned about video games and social media, did not grow up with smartphones or mobile computing devices and may not have a clear sense of how their children experience these technologies in their everyday lives and peer culture. Instead of focusing on learning about every new application, educators will benefit from learning about their group's overall experiences with technology. We suggest using the exercises early in this resource to just get a sense of what devices and applications students are using. If you have students who trust you to share this information, and if it is appropriate in your environment, you can ask students for a tour of some of the applications and online spaces they inhabit. For example, "Would you like to show me what you've built in your online game?" Or, "What kinds of photos do you like sharing with Instagram?"

Another challenge our students face is they are (knowingly or not) creating a digital footprint or impression of themselves that high schools, colleges, peers and future professional contacts may see. While we believe that some of the anxiety about these digital footprints is misplaced or overblown, we have also seen firsthand the social and emotional damage caused by out-of-context sharing of a romantic picture or a private text. The exercises in this curriculum encourage thoughtfulness, mindfulness and empathy. They encourage students to look inward and to their true support system for feedback on their identity, to avoid crowd-sourcing their identity and sense of self from social media.

Another challenge our students face is they are (knowingly or not) creating a digital footprint or impression of themselves that high schools, colleges, peers and future professional contacts may see.

We have tried all of the exercises in this book with different groups of young people. We've seen how eager young people are to have a space to talk and theorize about their digital experiences, rather than listen to a lecture about how they "abuse technology" or have "no boundaries." This curriculum stands out from others—giving students the space to reflect on their own experience, find empathy for themselves and their peers, and to make more positive choices from a more reflective place.

We wrote this curriculum because we passionately believe that young people need space to think through this part of their lives. This book can be used from beginning to end, or you can focus on the themes that are most relevant to a particular group of students at a specific time.

Guidelines for the Facilitator:

The lessons can be taught by any leader with youth experience in your community who genuinely likes children and appreciates their perspectives. It is helpful if the facilitator does not bring his/her own negative assumptions about the ways kids use technology.

NOTE: You don't need to be a tech expert to lead these exercises. We've provided a glossary that we will update online to help you, the facilitator, understand the format of the exercises and the terms young people use to talk about technology and to describe the apps and devices they most frequently use.

The goal of the curriculum is to get students thinking and talking about their experiences using digital media. The curriculum encourages discussion and activities. The facilitator can help by reading through the lesson prior to working with the students and thinking of real-life examples from other adults or students in the community. News articles also help make the material engaging and relevant.

The goal of the curriculum is to get students thinking and talking about their experiences using digital media.

The facilitator needs to create a safe space where students are comfortable sharing their thoughts, opinions, feelings and experiences. Safety is created by listening without judgment and encouraging differing opinions. Almost anyone who uses digital technology has made some kind of mistake; normalizing mistakes and encouraging dialogue about the incident can promote learning. Many of the discussion questions have no right answer; the facilitator encourages students to search their hearts, think about their values and formulate ideas about how they want to represent themselves and handle the situation. Students may share experiences where they or their friends have violated rules about technology. These real-life examples are valuable to explore and understand. Facilitators need to listen, not condemn, and be open to exploring why students made those choices and what the consequences are. Many online decisions are made impulsively, and students aren't thinking of the consequences. Just as in all relationships, communicating can be challenging, and kids will make mistakes. Online mistakes are opportunities for learning. Ideally, the facilitator has experience creating safe spaces where young people can share these sometimes vulnerable truths. They should be able to diffuse or carefully handle the ways students use these discussions to address issues with other students who are present in the room.

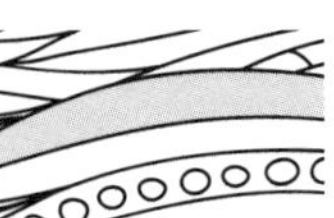

TOPIC 1:

Technology in Everyday Life

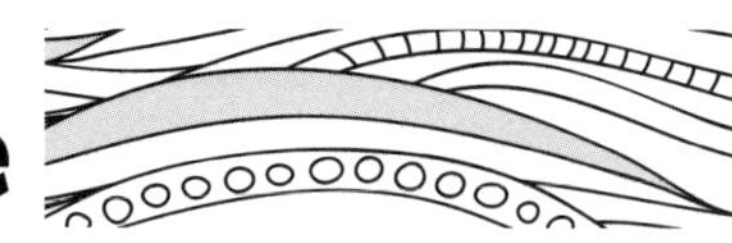

This section allows you, the educator, to understand more about the students in your learning community. Students will reflect on what technology, applications and content they are using on a day-to-day basis. The first exercise will show you and your students how these digital activities structure our lives, determining how we handle our time, eating, sleeping, school work, etc. The role of technology in mediating your students' peer relationships will also begin to emerge.

Lessons include:

Lesson 1:
Technology Inventory

Lesson 2:
Using Digital Technology Responsibly

Lesson 3:
Developing Guidelines with Technology

Lesson 4:
Family and Technology

The second exercise gives students a space to reflect on the rules—both spoken and unspoken—around technology at home, at school and in the wider community. This rules-focused exercise will help you design your school's digital citizenship curriculum and policies to make them as relevant as possible to your students' everyday experiences with the digital devices they use.

The final exercise in this chapter examines parents' roles in modeling media and technology use. Parents want what's best for their children, but their own limitations may prevent them from guiding their children in proper social media behavior. Further, they may be using technology themselves in ways that distract them from connecting with their children. Young people at many of the schools where we have worked have described how challenging it is just to get their parents' attention. Giving students a space to brainstorm solutions for this issue will help build community in your class. Discussions in this section will set the stage for later exercises in this curriculum.

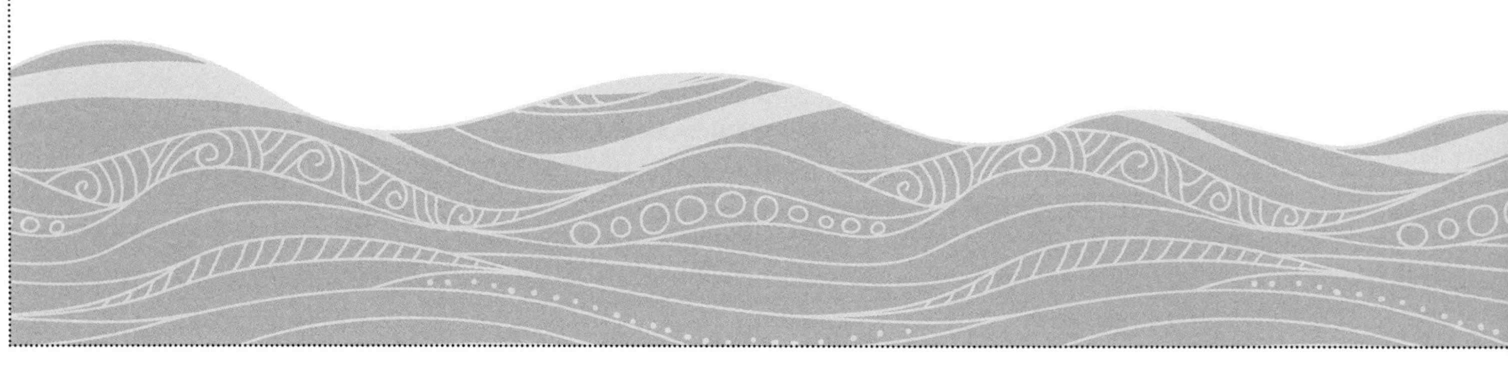

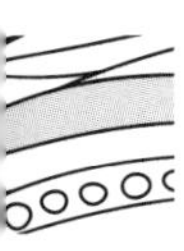

LESSON 1 | Technology Inventory

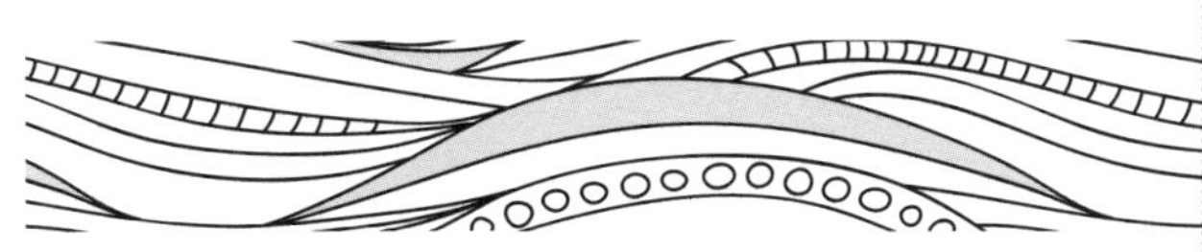

GOALS:

- To get a sense of how much technology each student is using and what type
- To have students examine the ways technology enhances their life as well as the concerns and mishaps that can occur

MATERIALS: Blank sheets of paper and writing utensils. HANDOUT: Map Your Digital Footprint

ACTIVITY: Give each student HANDOUT: Map Your Digital Footprint

1. Draw a map of your home. Draw where the technology is located. Place TVs, computers, ipads, iphones, itouches, handheld electronic games, online games, video games, Xbox, Wiis, Kindles, etc.
2. List the digital devices you use.
3. List the social networking sites you use.
4. Next to each device/site, write the age at which you received the digital device or were allowed to use the digital device.
5. Think about a typical day this week. Write down what you did from the time you woke up until bedtime. Total the number of hours or minutes you spent with a digital device.

Have students share their lists with a classmate.

Survey the class. Is there a wide variety in the number of digital devices? Is there a wide variety in amount of time students spend with screens?

ACTIVITY:

- Group students into groups of 4.
- Have each group list the advantages and positive things offered by digital communication tools. Have each group list the concerns, fears and misuses of digital communication tools.
- Write all the responses on the board.

DISCUSSION: Whole Group

Read each statement below. Have students comment on each statement.

- Kids between ages of 8-18 are using over 7 hours a day of media.
- Kids who have TV's and computers in the bedroom are at higher risk of obesity, sleep problems, increased aggression and academic problems.
- When kids play violent video games, they learn, rehearse and are rewarded for being violent. The message is that violence is the way to solve problems. Also kids become desensitized to violence.

- Kids who view violent media are more likely to be anxious, fearful, insensitive to others and aggressive.
- Kids tend to use technology as a way of managing their feelings. They disconnect from their feelings. They zone out.
- When kids use technology they are accustomed to being entertained by something else.
- When kids use technology they are less reliant on their own imagination.
- When kids use technology they are more easily bored.
- When kids use technology they are exposed to more mature content or language.

When kids play violent video games, they learn, rehearse and are rewarded for being violent. The message is that violence is the way to solve problems. Also kids become desensitized to violence.

ACTIVITY: Have students identify themselves as minimal digital users, moderate digital users or heavy digital users. This may vary throughout the week as some students are minimal users during the week and heavy users on the weekend. Challenge students to list the ways they can minimize how often they use technology and come up with ideas of what they would do instead of being "plugged in."

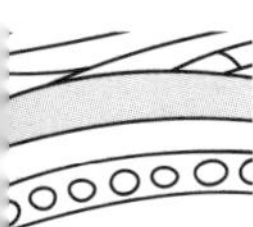

HANDOUT:

Map Your Digital Footprint

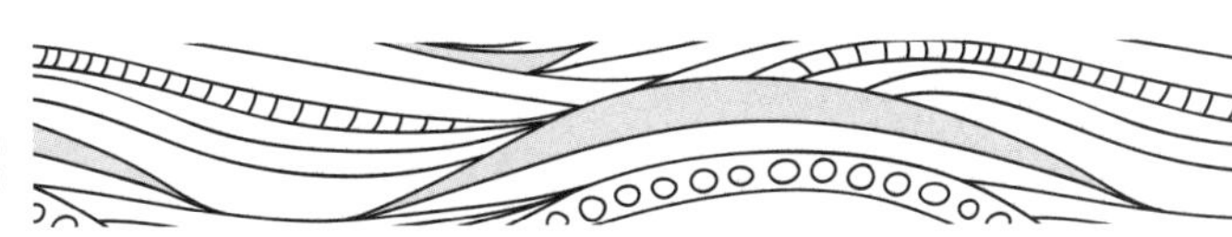

In the space below, draw a map of your home (you may draw 2 homes if your parents are divorced)

- List all the digital devices you use.
- List all the social networking sites you use.
- Next to each device/site, write the age at which you received the digital device or were allowed to use the digital device.
- In your drawing, place a star in all the spots in your house where you use the digital devices.

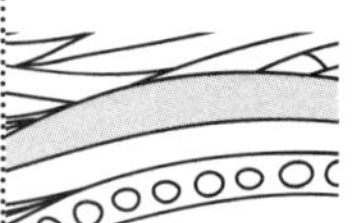

HANDOUT CONTINUED:

Map Your Digital Footprint

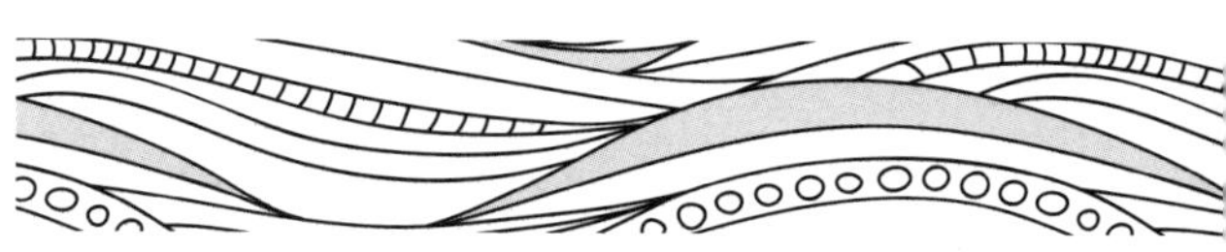

Think about a typical day this week. Think about when you use any digital devices and for how long from the moment you woke up until you went to bed. Complete the chart below. If on Monday morning before school, you played 20 minutes of a digital game on the ipad and then responded to a text and an instant message, you might put 22 minutes into the box 7-8 a.m. on Monday.

Total the number of hours or minutes you spent with a screen for each day.

When are you the most digitally active? Which days, which times? Why?

Day of week	Sunday	Monday	Tuesday	Wednesday	Thursday	Friday	Saturday
6-7 am							
7-8 am							
8-9 am							
9-10 am							
10-11 am							
11-12 pm							
12-1 pm							
1-2 pm							
2-3 pm							
3-4 pm							
4-5 pm							
5-6 pm							
6-7 pm							
7-8 pm							
8-9 pm							
9-10 pm							
10-11 pm							
11-12 am							

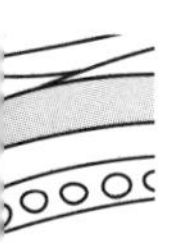

LESSON 2 | Using Digital Technology Responsibly

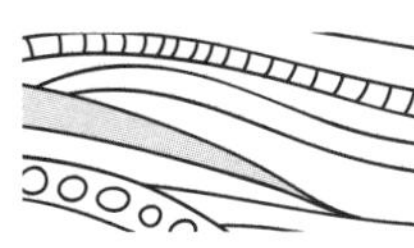

GOALS:

- To encourage students to understand the difference between appropriate and inappropriate usage of various types of technology
- To identify problematic behavior of peers and others
- To foster respectful and safe behavior when using digital media
- To help students represent themselves and others in a respectful, responsible manner

MATERIALS: None

ACTIVITY: Brainstorm with students some of the problems they have seen occurring with the use of digital technology? (Write all answers on a board, encourage students to be specific)

- People giving out passwords
- Not saving work
- Hacking accounts
- Personal information getting out to public
- Not sure of who you are having conversations with – people are not who they say they are and it can be dangerous
- Using technology when you should be doing something else
- Tempting to go on other sites
- Time consuming
- Write things in text or email that you didn't mean
- Write things in text or email and send it to wrong person
- Post a picture that gets you in trouble or offends someone
- Reader/viewer does not understand tone and gets upset
- Easy to post offensive thing anonymously
- Hurt feelings
- Cyberbullying – way to tease or exclude, way to insult someone or gang up on them without them knowing
- Parents and teachers usually don't know what is going on
- Post things impulsively, that you later regret

BRAINSTORM: What are broad categories of misuse of technology? Group behaviors. (Example: mean behavior, unsafe behavior, harassing behavior, etc)

ACTIVITY: STEP IN (or Stand Up)
Have students get in a circle (or remain sitting where they are). Students will take one step into the circle (or stand up) if the statement is true for them. Instruct students to simply observe who and how many are in the circle (or standing up) and who and how many are not. There is no right or wrong. You can allow for discussion after each question or wait and discuss at the end.

STEP IN/STAND UP if:

- You have ever sent a text, email, picture, message to the wrong person
- You have ever made a post you wish you could take back
- You have ever sent a text, email picture, message, made a move in a game that was misunderstood – that you know upset someone even though you didn't mean to...
- You have ever sent a text, email picture, message, made a move in a game that you would never want your parents to see
- You have received a text, email, picture, message or were gaming and someone did/said something that hurt your feelings
- You have received a text, email, picture, message that made you cringe... that you knew was inappropriate in some way
- You have received a text, email, picture, message that you knew would hurt someone else's feelings
- You have had a friend that texted you too many times
- You have had a friend that got upset if you did not respond to a text

DISCUSSION: How does it feel when you realize that your post hurt someone's feelings or was misunderstood?

- Do you always know feelings were hurt?
- How do you fix it? Is it easy?
- Has a text, email, or post ever created a big problem?
- Do your parents check your emails, texts, posts, etc? Have they ever told you that certain posts were inappropriate? How do you handle it?
- When have you been bothered or upset with things that others have posted about you or sent to you?
- What do you do when you are upset about something online?

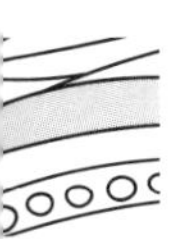

LESSON 3: Developing Guidelines with Technology

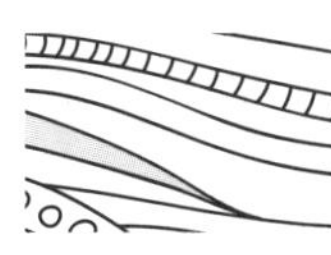

- To empower children to think about their relationship with technology
- To foster students to set appropriate boundaries for themselves and with their peers
- To offer a space for critical engagement with family/ school / community technology rules or guidelines

MATERIALS: White board or large paper
Stickers/Markers of different colors

BRAINSTORM: Ask students, "What are some of the rules your parents have set for you about using digital media?" (List on white board or paper – the more rules the better.)

ACTIVITY:

- Provide each student three stickers/ markers of different colors. (Students can use three markers of different colors if stickers are not available.)
- Each student should place a green sticker/marker on the rules that you believe are good rules and promote safe and responsible use.
- Each student should place a red sticker/marker on rules they disagree with.
- Each student should place a yellow sticker/marker on rules that are hard to follow.
- Have students discuss the reasons they marked each the way they did.

ACTIVITY: If the school has a set of rules about technology, distribute copies of the rules. Have students take turns reading rules aloud.

Discuss:

- Which rules are hard to follow? Why?
- Which rules do students violate? Why?
- Are there any rules that are missing that students feel should be on the list?

BRAINSTORM: If the school does not have a clear set of rules/guidelines about technology, have students brainstorm ideas of what the rules could be. Go back to Lesson 1 for ideas.

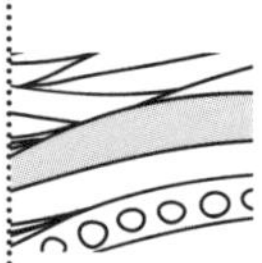

LESSON 4 | Family and Technology

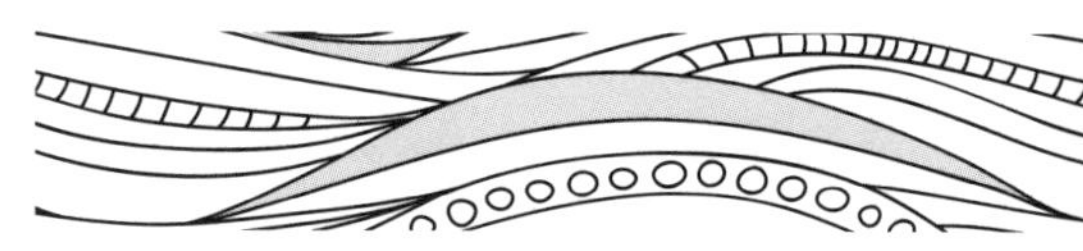

GOALS:

- To provide students with a place to reflect on their parents'/guardians' cellphone and computer usage
- To help students understand that everyone needs limits with technology

MATERIALS: Whiteboard or large sheets of paper

BRAINSTORM: Ask students to name behaviors that their parents engage in with technology that are annoying or even dangerous (texting at dinner, texting while driving, taking calls during family time, posting pics of their kids without kids' permission).

As a group, develop a list of these behaviors. If you have time, you can have students demonstrate the behaviors with short skits.

Ask students to raise their hand if they believe someone in their family uses technology too much. Ask for volunteers to share how technology has had an impact on their family.

ACTIVITY:

App Design Challenge: Working in small groups, have students design an app to control or eradicate the annoying or concerning parental behavior. Students should come up with a name for the app, draw the icon for the app, and describe what the application does to change behavior. Allow at least 20 minutes for this process.

In the next 20-30 minutes, or in a subsequent session, have each group present their app. Students should introduce the application, show the images they have created and explain how the application changes parent behavior. If you choose, they may act out a commercial where the app is demonstrated.

You can do an applause-o-meter or offer prizes to the top two apps, or all of the apps!

*If students are more advanced, allow them to ask questions and iterate/improve their apps after the presentation. You can also ask them about who the app is marketed towards and what kind of research they would do. Would parents choose this app? How would we sell to them without making them feel like "bad parents."

DISCUSSION:

- What are criteria that make parents like an app?
- What are criteria that make kids like an app? How would you market your app?

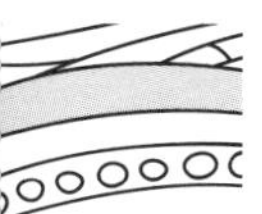

TOPIC 2:

Texting Challenges

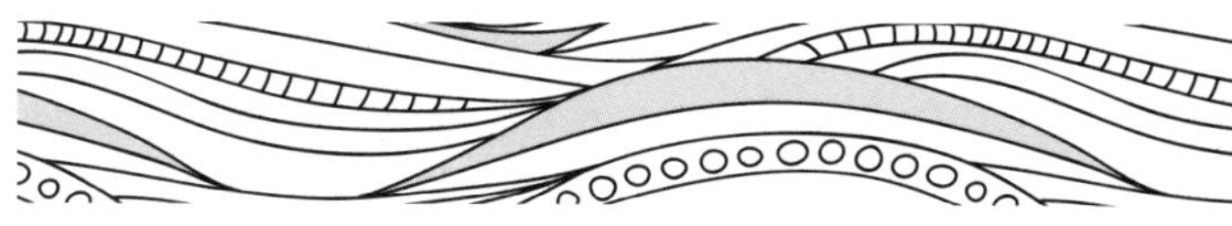

Digital devices in the hands of our kids come with many more opportunities for miscommunication. Tensions between friends can arise from something as minor as an unanswered text message. Young people need to understand that instant messaging isn't always instant. We need to let kids know that this is OK—that whether you are in 6th grade or a grownup, when people don't answer our texts right away, they are probably busy eating, doing homework etc, not ignoring us! Since texts also arrive without other context, kids need help managing emotions around texts, and when addressing a situation where in-person communication is more appropriate than texting.

Lessons include:

Lesson 5:
Text Misunderstandings and Mishaps

Lesson 6:
Text and Tone (Preventing Misunderstandings)

Lesson 7:
Resolving Texting Problems

As students begin to text one another, several challenges present themselves. One challenge is related to knowing when to text. With a telephone in a central location in homes, many of today's adults grew up with defined boundaries around calling times. The understanding that it was rude to call during the dinner hour or after a certain time of night was a widely shared understanding. Because texting is perceived as less disruptive, and because each family member may have his or her own device, the rules and boundaries for when and how often to text are less clear. Kids need help navigating this. It may be helpful to encourage parents to make sure their children aren't texting late into the night, for example. Furthermore, the interpersonal conflicts that you remember as a child are all still there, but the landscape has changed. Digital devices and texting add opportunities for miscommunication. Tensions between friends can arise from something as minor as an unanswered text message. These exercises will help students understand that instant messaging and texting isn't always instant. They will help your students create and assert appropriate boundaries and to have more realistic expectations.

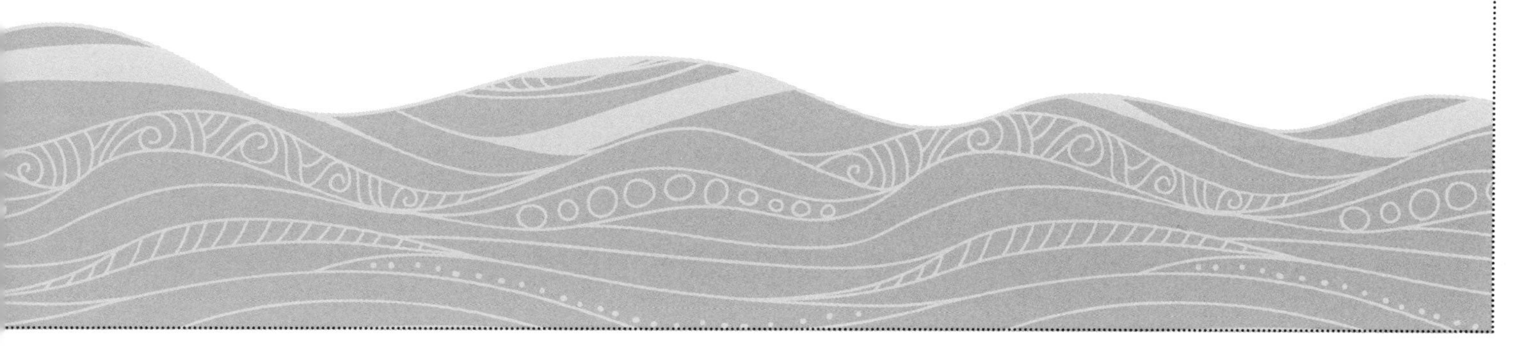

LESSON 5 | Text Misunderstandings and Mishaps

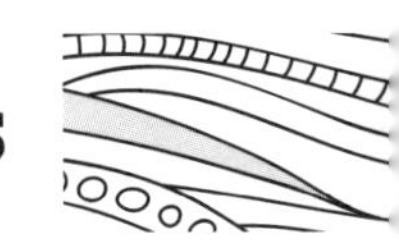

- To encourage students to respect other people's time and boundaries
- To encourage students to empathize with the recipient of their texts

MATERIALS: Index cards with questions written on them (optional):
Sign with "Strongly Disagree" written on it
Sign with "Strongly Agree" written on it

ACTIVITY: Have students line up in two lines. Have a student from each line come forward. Read one of the questions below to the two students. Instruct the two students to debate the question out loud in front of the whole group for 2-3 minutes and come up with a joint answer.

- How long is it OK to wait to respond to a text?
- How long is it OK to wait to respond to a voicemail?
- Is it ever OK to send a text while you are:
  - in class?
  - at lunch with friends?
  - with your family at breakfast?
  - at church or synagogue?
  - at night when you are supposed to be sleeping?
  - at a friend's house?
  - in the bathroom?

ACTIVITY: Place cards with the words "Strongly Disagree" at one end of the room and the words "Strongly Agree" at the other side of the room. Ask students to stand under the sign that describes how they feel about each statement:

- I will text right before class/lunch/breakfast/church if it is REALLY important
- I will text again if I text someone and they don't text back within 5 minutes
- I think that if someone doesn't text back, they are rude
- Waiting for someone to text back is very difficult for me
- If someone doesn't text back, I think they are mad at me

DISCUSSION:

- How do you feel if someone texts you 5 times without waiting for a response?
- How do you feel if you can't respond to a text?

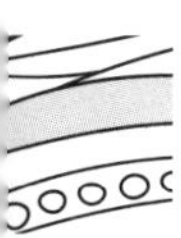

LESSON 6 | Text and Tone (Preventing Misunderstandings)

GOALS:

- To learn and understand common terms, abbreviations and symbols used in online communication
- To help students understand how easily texts, posts, emails and other digital communication can be misinterpreted
- To increase consciousness of how others may perceive words and actions
- To prevent hurt feelings

MATERIALS: Handout: Netspeak
Index cards or small strips of paper

ACTIVITY: Divide students into groups of 3-4. Have students complete Handout 2.6, defining the netspeak terms. Ask the group:

- How many of you knew all of the netspeak terms?
- How many of you knew at least 10 terms?
- How many of you knew less than 10 terms?
- Are there other popular terms that are used frequently by your group?
- Discuss the reasons for using netspeak and when you should use it.

ACTIVITY: Distribute small slips of paper to each student. Direct each student to write a statement that could be interpreted either as friendly or sarcastic. Have students submit the paper to you. Examples include:

- Nice hair, JK
- Can't believe we are partners, LOL
- You like her?
- Whatever

Have students form 2 even lines (LINE A and LINE B). Pick one of the statements listed on the small pieces of paper. Have the first persons in each line come forward and look at the statement. The person from LINE A needs to interpret the statement in a friendly way, reading the sentence with a friendly tone to the class. The first person in LINE B needs to interpret the sentence in a sarcastic way, reading it with a mean tone. Discuss. Move to the next two people in each line.

HANDOUT:

Netspeak

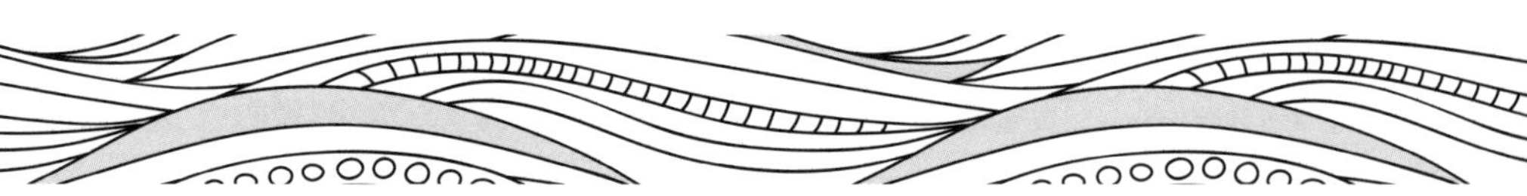

Write the definition to each term:

BRB ______________________________

Code 9 (CD 9) ______________________________

GTG______________________________

MIRL______________________________

LOL______________________________

IDK ______________________________

S2R ______________________________

W/E______________________________

POS______________________________

MOS ______________________________

DOS ______________________________

P911 ______________________________

PIR ______________________________

Noob______________________________

IMO ______________________________

YOLO ______________________________

Trolling______________________________

List other terms commonly used by your peers:

____

____

____

____

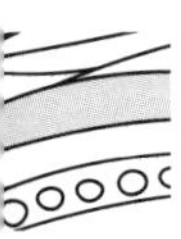

LESSON 7 | Resolving Texting Problems

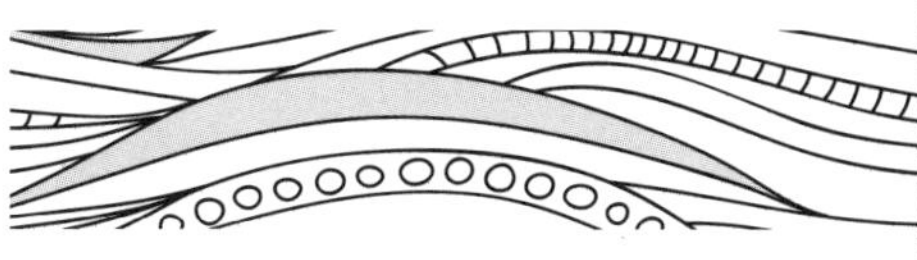

GOALS:

- To increase awareness of the impact of texting one friend repeatedly when he/she is not responding
- To explore the challenges of group texts
- To help students problem solve around texting etiquette
- To increase student's empathy for others and prevent texting impatience and rudeness

BRAINSTORM: Brainstorm a list of things someone could be doing other than answering your text. Examples include: taking a shower, homework, talking with another friend, eating with family, attending a religious service, sleeping (let students come up with the ideas).

DISCUSSION: Have students think about a time when they sent a text and wanted an immediate response but did not get one. Have them remember how they felt and what they were thinking. Ask students to share their feelings and thoughts with the students sitting near them.

Often people feel they need an immediate response. Often we do not understand the delay especially if we had just been in contact with our friend. Sometimes we assume our friend ignored us. Other times we do not need an immediate response. Give friends time and space online as you would in real life.

Ask students to share other annoying or problematic behaviors they have experienced in their engagement with texting; group texts, thoughtless texts, misunderstandings, etc.

ACTIVITY: App Design Challenge

Assign students to work in small groups to design an app that solves a texting problem. Group size should be determined by the class size divided by how many presentations you will have time for at the end. Students should draw their app's icon and an image of what the app looks like when you are using it. Their app should have a name and a list of functions. If students are more advanced, allow them to ask questions and iterate/improve their apps after the presentation. You can also ask them about who the app is marketed towards and what kind of research they would do. If you have more time, they can also create a commercial for their app.

Examples of texting problems include: the friend who sends too many texts, group texting challenges, the friend who gets hurt when you don't respond.

Have students present their app to the group. You can offer prizes, an applause-o-meter or some other fun way to increase competition if that works well with this group. You can also avoid competition completely. You can also do an entire session on design and a follow-up session with presentations if time allows.

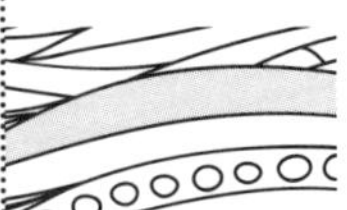

TOPIC 3:

Social Media/Socializing Online

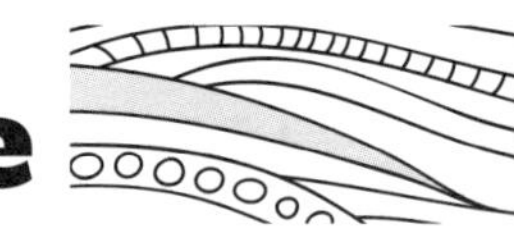

Social media includes applications like Facebook, Instagram, Snapchat, Keek and Vine, as well as websites where young people interact, such as ask.fm. Many social media spaces are intended for people aged 13 and up, but in our experience this age limit is rarely observed and easy to circumvent, simply by stating a different age or birthdate. Adults use social media differently than young people. Social media is a space where young people can "hang out," even when they are not with their friends. Young teens' and tweens' identities are in flux, so they are especially attracted to the ever-changing nature of social media photo communication applications like Snapchat. Applications such as Facebook can still be attractive, but the long memory of a Facebook "wall" may be one of the reasons that Facebook is losing popularity among 13-17 year olds.

Lessons include:

Lesson 8:
Privacy/ What Not to Share

Lesson 9:
Feeling Left Out/ Being Inclusive

Lesson 10:
Being a Friend vs. a "Friend"/"Follower"

Some students may go to sites such as Omegle to talk to strangers, but for the most part they are interested in interacting with other kids they already know or who are at least connected to people they know in person. Social media feels like a peer space. One of the challenges of social media is that kids forget who they are communicating with; they may only keep in mind small segments of their potential audience. Thus they sometimes share things intended for a few of their friends and forget that their parents, or a wider peer group, might see what they share. Interestingly, sometimes a student is angry or feels violated when those unintended people comment or react, even though the student was the one who shared the image or text. Another challenge of social media is "friend curation," knowing who to "follow" or "friend" on a service.

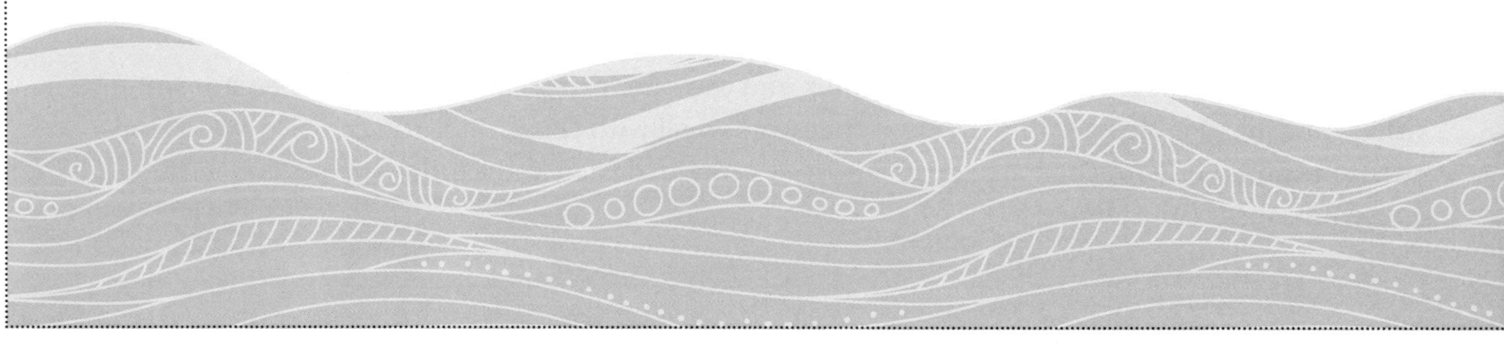

LESSON 8 | Privacy: What Not to Share

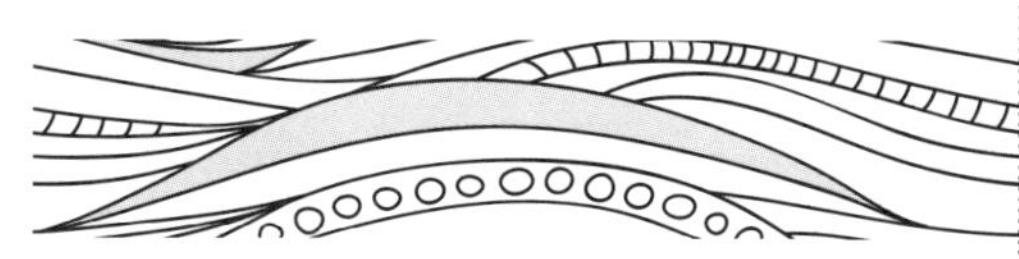

- To get students to realize about the public nature of online communication
- To foster mindfulness and decrease impulsivity so students will think about the feelings of others before posting

MATERIALS: Tape

ACTIVITY: Step In (Stand Up) – activity explained on page 13, Lesson 2.

- Your mom/dad shared something about you that you didn't like.
- Your parents shared a picture of you that you wish they had not shared.
- A friend shared something about you that you wish they had not.
- Someone has posted your news before you were ready to share it.
- You shared something by mistake that was supposed to be a secret.
- You shared someone's secret on purpose.
- Someone showed you someone else's texts on their phone.
- You looked at someone's texts on their phone without them knowing.
- A parent, classmate or teacher looked at the texts on your phone.

ACTIVITY: Place a piece of masking tape across the floor. Explain that one end of the tape is where you stand if something really bothers you and the other end of the tape is where you would stand if something would not bother you at all.

Read each statement and have students think about how they would feel if this happened to them. Stand on the tape to show the degree of your feeling. Discuss before moving on to next statement.

Totally Bothered | Would Not Care At All

"How bothered would you be by having the following information posted:"

- Having low test scores
- Having high test scores
- Who you were going to ask to a dance
- Relationship status posted
- Parents getting divorced
- Parent losing a job
- Getting a part in a play

- Where you got into high school (if relevant at your school)
- How much money your parents make
- That you see a therapist/dermatologist/dietitian
- That you kissed a certain person at a party
- Your sexual orientation
- Your best friend's sexual orientation

DISCUSSION

- What kind of pictures should be private?
- What are some things that other people share that make you uncomfortable/wish they would keep to themselves?
- What's a time when someone shared something about you that you thought should be private?
- How do you know if it is OK to share news/ or a picture?

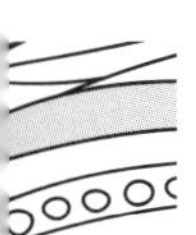

LESSON 9 | Feeling Left Out: Being Inclusive

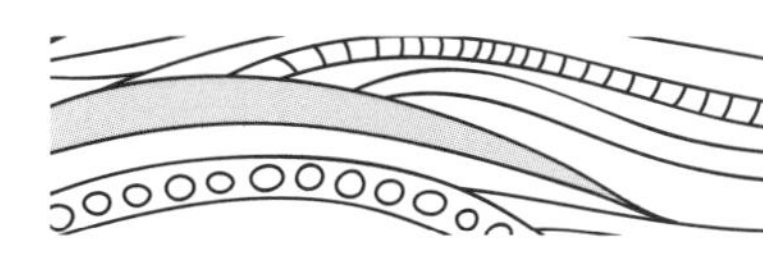

- To help students focus on being more present, and recognize the universality of the challenge that FOMO (fear of missing out) presents
- To help students realize the impact of the things they write and post
- To help students manage their own feelings of being left out

MATERIALS: Images of kids together having fun, this can be pictures from magazines or pictures from internet. Images can be projected on white board or smart board or can be cut and pasted on to poster board. Signs with the words "NO," "IT DEPENDS," "YES" on them.

DISCUSSION: Show an image of peers having fun together, at an event together, celebrating together. Ask students how this picture could make someone feel bad.

ACTIVITY: Have students get into groups of 2 or 3. Instruct the groups to:

- Describe a time that you felt left out because of something you saw on Instagram.
- Describe a time that you thought about not posting something because you worried that other people might feel left out.
- What are some things you can do if you are looking at Instagram and you feel this way?
- Do you ever feel like if you take a break from your phone that you might miss something really important?
- Do you think people ever post pictures of themselves having fun with other friends on purpose to make others feel left out?
- What might someone gain from doing this?
- Describe a time you felt left out looking at a picture.

ACTIVITY: Have signs with the words "NO," "IT DEPENDS," "YES" posted around the room. Read each question and ask students to take a stand under the sign that best describes how they feel. Discuss their choices.

- Can you post pictures of your birthday party where only half of the class was invited?
- Can you post your 100% on your major exam?
- Can you post a picture of your friend's birthday party where only half of the class is invited?
- You have a lot of close friends. Can you post a picture of you and a friend and say "Me and my BFF!"

ACTIVITY: Divide students into two groups. Have one group write up posts that can hurt others and the other group write up posts that can encourage others.

DISCUSSION: Are there times it is best not share images? How can you help a friend who feels left out?

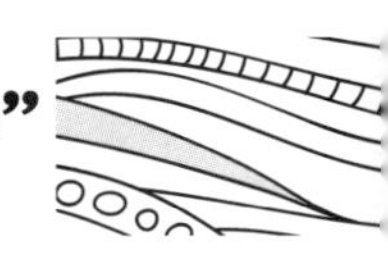

LESSON 10 | Being a Friend vs. a "Friend"/"Follower"

GOALS:

- To get students to articulate what it takes to be a true friend
- To encourage students to articulate their criteria for who follows them, who they follow in social media
- To explore whether it is rude or appropriate to ignore a friend request, or not to "follow back" someone

MATERIALS: Sheets of lined paper.

ACTIVITY: Have each student fold a piece of notebook paper in half to create two columns. On the left side, have students list things that true friends do. On the right side, have students list things that true friends don't do.

Collect the lists. List some qualities on the board. Spend some time discussing these qualities.

DISCUSSION: Have students think about the categories of people they are connected to via social media. Ask students:

- How many friends or followers do they have?
- Does the amount of friends matter?
- How many of their connections would they consider "True Friends"?
- How many are acquaintances?
- How many followers are people they don't know?
- Why do you choose to follow people you do not know?
- When is it OK to "unfriend" or "unfollow" someone?

ACTIVITY: Debate

Ask students to volunteer to debate both sides of the following statements:

- Is it rude to not "follow back" or to ignore a "friend request"?
- It is rude not to friend someone, if they ask you.
- It is rude not to friend someone, if you have met them.
- It is rude not to friend someone, if they know your friends.
- If a friend posts something, do you feel like you need to like it or comment?

TOPIC 4:

Visual Communication: Online Images

Today's young people are very tuned in to visual communication. In social media spaces, many young people are communicating through photographs and video. Tumblr, Instagram and Vine are predominantly visual spaces, though text and narrative can also be important. In many cases, not only is a picture worth a thousand words, pictures can be more influential (and sometimes more damaging) than those thousand words.

Lessons include:

Lesson 11:
Interpreting Online Images of Peers

Lesson 12:
Ask First: Every Day is Picture Day

Lesson 13:
Beauty is Only Skin Deep: Body Image and Social Media

Young people are navigating social media beauty contests, where peers may post a group of girls and ask for votes to see who is the least attractive, whittling down the selection to one "winner" and reducing all the girls to images. "Stud Contests" commit the same damaging actions with boys' pictures. Needless to say, everyone loses in this kind of interaction—the children or teens pictured, their peers who vote or see them in this way, and everyone who does not intervene. Letting young people know they can take a stand against beauty contests is one way to empower them to resist this damaging practice.

Another challenge young people face is feeling left out because they see images of peers socializing without them. It is one thing to learn about something you missed after the fact, but it is even more painful to watch photos being posted in real time while a party or get together is taking place without you.

Yet another challenge is being judged by their clothes, hair, tattoos or other aspects of their physical appearance. While this can happen in person, photo sharing in social media means that young people are often in a position to quickly judge one another from a photograph, without even having met. Young people are also intentionally forming their identities through online image sharing, so they may perform in certain ways on social media that they would hesitate to do in everyday life. While social media can be a place to try on sexuality, gender identity, or simply new fashion, young people need to know that these explorations are not private.

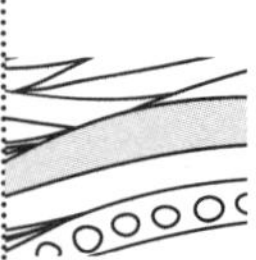

LESSON 11 | Interpreting Online Images of Peers

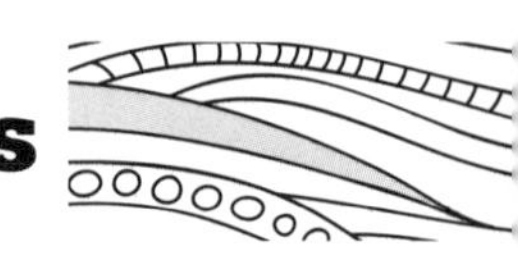

GOALS:

- To increase awareness of the assumptions students make based on photographs
- To help students understand their own self-representation
- To help students be mindful about when and what to share and to understand that once something is shared, the individual no longer has control of that information

MATERIALS: Images on page 30. Device to project images or printed hard copies of photographs

Other images that you think will resonate with the group of students you are working with as well as images of students that are different from the students you are working with.

ACTIVITY: Have students divide up into groups of 4-5. Let them know that small group discussion will be followed by sharing, but they don't need to write things down.

Distribute or project the first image: (Girl with A's on her report card)

- What do you think is going on in this picture?
- What impression are they trying create?
- Who posted it? Why?
- If this was someone you know, would think about this photo differently?

Distribute or project the 2nd image: ("Tough-looking" boy)

- What is your opinion of the boy in this image?
- What do you think he wants you to think about him?
- Who posted it? Why?
- If this was someone you know, would you think about this photo differently?

Distribute or project the 3rd image: (selfie – boy looking depressed)

- What do you think is going on with the guy in this picture?
- What does his photo say to you?
- Who posted it? Why?
- If this was someone you know, would you think about this photo differently?

Distribute or project the 4rd image: (Girl trying to look sexy)

- What do you think about this girl from seeing this picture?
- What do think this girl wants others to think of her?
- Who posted it? Why?
- If this was someone you know, would you think about this photo differently?

DISCUSSION: How do people make assumptions about others based on a photo that was posted of them? Let's look back at one of the photos.

- What do we actually know about these students?
- What are we inferring?
- Is it fair? Why is it so different when you know someone?
- Why is it so different if someone posts something themselves vs. if their mom posts it?
- How would your assumptions change if this was a picture of a friend?

Have students turn to the person next to them to discuss the following:

- Have you ever seen someone's profile and thought that person was not cool, weird, or not the kind of person you would like, then you met the person and he/she was not how he/she seemed in the picture?

Have you ever seen someone's profile that you really thought was cool, then you met the person and they are not how they seemed in the picture?

- Have you thought someone you know was presenting a totally fake image of themselves online?
- Do you think your digitally posted photos accurately reflect who you are?
- Can photographs ever reflect who we really are?
- What would you say is your online reputation?

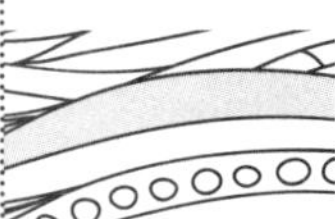

HANDOUT:

Social Media Photos

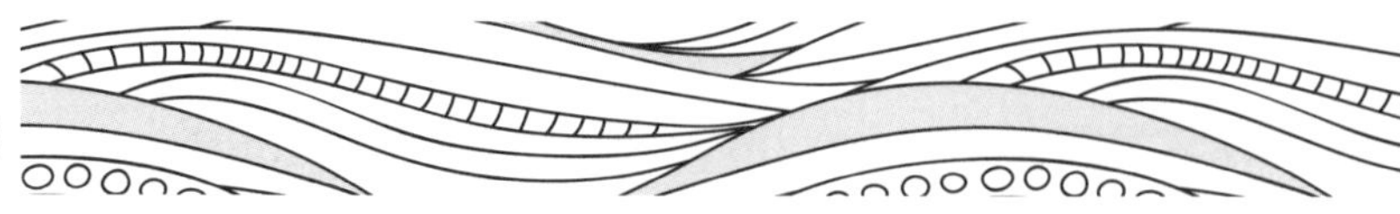

1

2

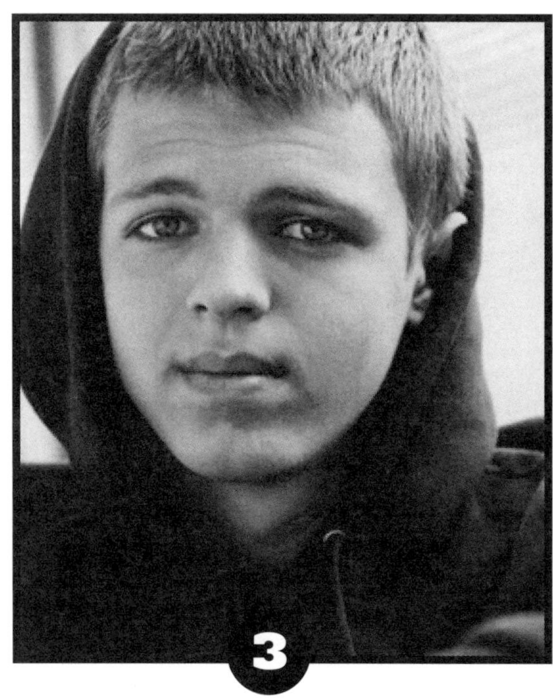

3

4

LESSON 12 | Ask First: Every Day is Picture Day

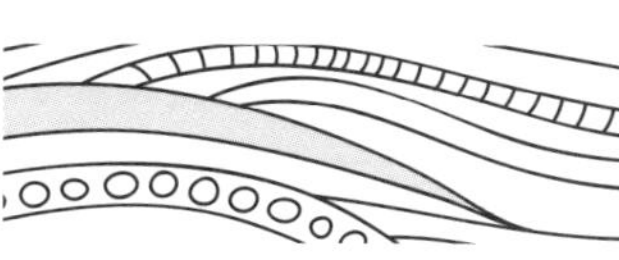

GOALS:

- To make students aware that they should ask permission before taking or sharing photographs
- To help students understand their own self-representation
- To increase mindfulness about when and what to share and to understand that once something is shared, the individual no longer has control of that information

MATERIALS: Copies of HANDOUT: Every Day is Picture Day

Photographs on page 30

Device to project images or printed hard copies of photographs

Other images that you think will resonate with the group of students you are working with as well as images of students that are different from the students you are working with.

ACTIVITY: Have the students complete the handout.

Collect handouts and graph or present the results. Discuss the results with the entire class.

DISCUSSION: Think about a time someone took your picture without consent. How did it feel? How did you respond?

How do we behave when we know we might be photographed vs. when we are not likely to be photographed?

Today's young people are very tuned in to visual communication. Pictures can be more influential, and sometimes more damaging, than those thousand words.

HANDOUT:

Every Day is Picture Day

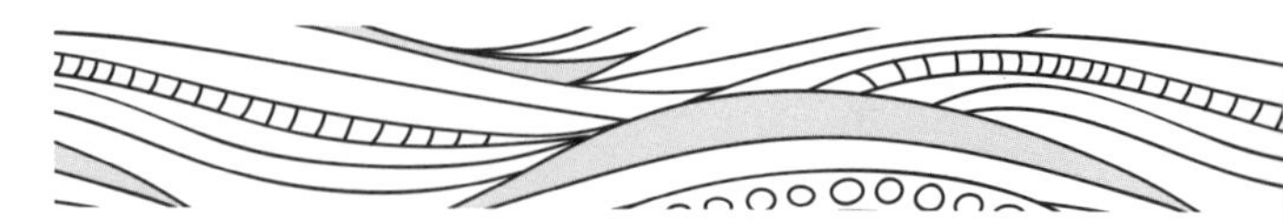

Agreement Rating Sheet:

0 = Strongly Disagree 1= Disagree 2= Unsure 3= Agree 4= Strongly Agree

> People should ask each other before taking a picture of them.

0 1 2 3 4

> People should get a friend or classmate's permission before sharing their photograph.

0 1 2 3 4

> People share pictures all the time without permission.

0 1 2 3 4

> I don't really care if someone shares my picture.

0 1 2 3 4

> I feel embarrassed or angry when an unflattering picture of me is posted.

0 1 2 3 4

> Sometimes it is stressful to be photographed.

0 1 2 3 4

> Since everyone takes so many pictures, I feel like I have to look my best.

0 1 2 3 4

> Is it okay to take photos in your underclothing?

0 1 2 3 4

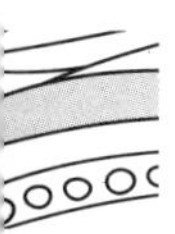

LESSON 13

Beauty is Only Skin Deep: Body Image and Social Media

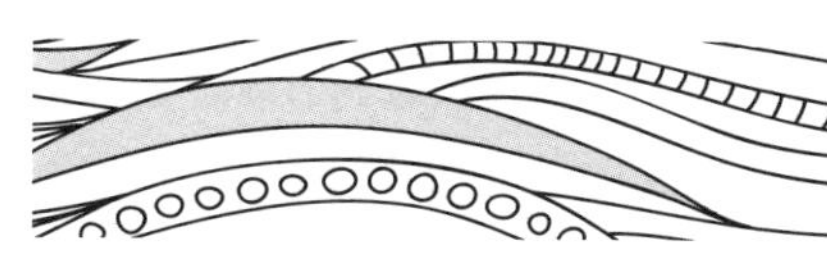

GOALS:

- To give students a place to reflect on the way we judge ourselves and others based on images
- To increase awareness that photos are altered and enhanced

MATERIALS: Copies of HANDOUT: The Meaning of Pictures

Computer to show class YouTube video: www.youtube.com/watch?v=hibyAJOSW8U

ACTIVITY: Have students complete HANDOUT: The Meaning of Pictures. Discuss results.

Show class YouTube Video "Evolution of Beauty – Dove Campaign for Real Beauty." Have students share their reactions to video.

DISCUSSION: Divide students into groups of 4-5. Ask students to discuss the following questions:

- How did you choose your profile picture?
- How often do you change your profile picture?
- What does your profile picture say about you?

ACTIVITY: Poster Design

Ask students if they have ever seen a beauty contest online? Have students describe beauty contests they have experienced online so that everyone in the group has a shared understanding of what they are.

- Discuss the downsides of beauty contests. How would you feel if presented with a beauty contest?
- Discuss possible snappy retorts you could use if presented with a beauty contest.
- Have students work in small groups to design a poster/ad that discourages negative beauty contests online.

HANDOUT:

The Meaning of Pictures

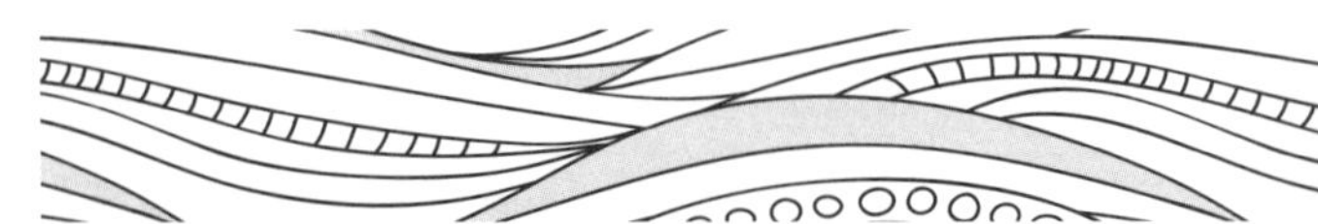

Read each statement and rate the degree to which you agree or disagree.

Agreement Rating Sheet:

0 = Strongly Disagree 1= Disagree 2= Unsure 3= Agree 4= Strongly Agree

1) I love taking selfies.

0 1 2 3 4

2) I hate looking at pictures of myself.

0 1 2 3 4

3) Sometimes I judge people by how they look in pictures, but when I meet them I am surprised.

0 1 2 3 4

4) If you follow me online you will get a good sense of my true personality.

0 1 2 3 4

5) I feel judged by how I look?

0 1 2 3 4

6) If your friends wanted you to meet someone, would you want to see pictures online first?

0 1 2 3 4

7 I'd prefer if people asked before they tag me in a picture.

0 1 2 3 4

8) I hate when people post pictures of me when I look bad.

0 1 2 3 4

9) I love to post ugly selfies.

0 1 2 3 4

10) Sometimes people post pictures of themselves just to get a compliment.

0 1 2 3 4

11) I've seen students post mean comments on how other students look or dress.

0 1 2 3 4

12) I've had people post mean comments on how I look/what I am wearing.

0 1 2 3 4

13) Girls care more about how they look than boys.

0 1 2 3 4

14) Girls are more judgmental about how others look than boys.

0 1 2 3 4

TOPIC 5:

Mean on Screen: Bullying, Drama and Thoughtlessness

While many educators are aware of cyberbullying, in this section we address a wide continuum of unkind and difficult behaviors, ranging from perceived slights to thoughtless unkindness to intentional drama and gossip, even to the ways that severe face-to-face bullying can extend into other forms of communication like email, texting or social media. Part of the challenge with drama and thoughtlessness is that the rules and expectations for who can and how to share information are still evolving.

Lessons include:

Lesson 14:
Avoiding Drama

Lesson 15:
Mean-ness vs. Drama vs. Bullying

Lesson 16:
Preventing Cyberbullying: Using the screen to be mean

Lesson 17:
The Ups and Downs of Anonymity

Lesson 18:
To Tell or Not to Tell

Gossip can spread more quickly on social media or via text or group chat, but the existence of gossip is as old as human community. Likewise, bullying has been part of school communities forever, but social media, texting and hand-held devices give students more access to one another to cause harm.

Our lesson on anonymity is very important as students need to understand the dynamics that anonymity can create and reinforce, as well as understand that if they are bullied anonymously, they are dealing with especially cowardly behavior. While bullying is never the target's fault, students should be aware that creating profiles in anonymous spaces makes them vulnerable to these kinds of attacks. The exercises and discussions help empower students to stand up to mean-spirited, hurtful activity online and seek help from a trusted adult if they witness or experience any form of bullying behavior.

LESSON 14 | Avoiding Drama

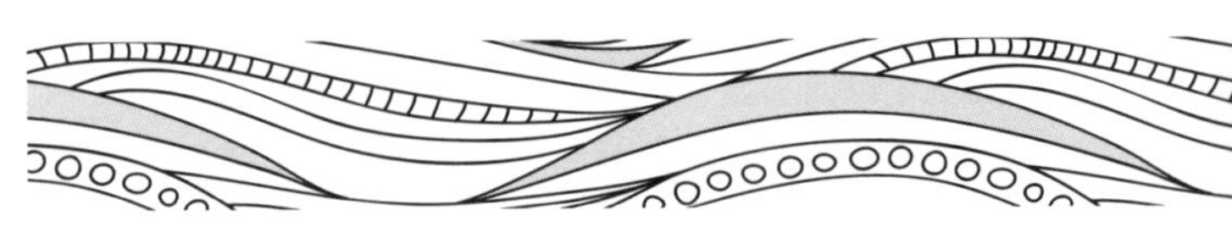

GOALS:

- To give students confidence in their ability to problem solve around conflict
- To provide students tools to fix interpersonal challenges without making them worse

MATERIALS: Scenario cards (cut apart)

ACTIVITY: Group Brainstorming

Pair students up and provide each pair a different scenario card. Have the pair brainstorm the best responses to their situation. With the entire group, have each pair discuss their situation and what they thought was the best response. Discuss with the group if they have any other suggestions.

Continue until most of the scenarios have been addressed.

BRAINSTORM: Ask all students to brainstorm ideas on how people can avoid texting problems, misunderstandings and drama. Have these ideas posted or displayed somewhere.

DISCUSSION:

- What are the challenges to resolving a conflict?
- What makes it easier to resolve?
- Provide steps you could take to avoid any drama with friends.
- Is it easier to resolve conflicts in person or in a text?
- How would you approach someone face-to-face to resolve a conflict?

While bullying is never the target's fault, students should be aware that creating profiles in anonymous spaces makes them vulnerable to these kinds of attacks.

HANDOUT:

Scenario Cards

You write a text about a private matter and send it to the wrong people.	You are mad at your friend and send a hostile text, saying "I can't believe you did that to me. You're not my friend..."
You are mad at a friend so you post a nasty picture.	You said something about someone in a text to your friend. Your friend forwarded the comment.
Your parent looks at your texts and sees that a friend has been using inappropriate language and suggesting that you lie to your parents. You have told your friend not to send you those kinds of texts but he/she does it anyway. Now your parents are taking your phone away.	You make a comment to a friend about another friend. It is just a joke. You would never want to hurt someone's feelings. Your friend misinterprets the text and tells the other friend.

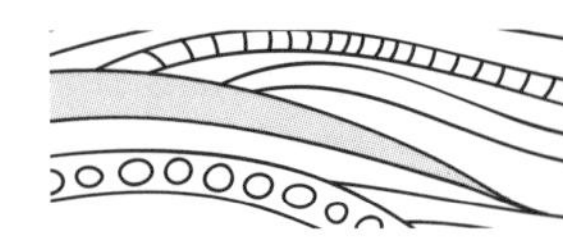

LESSON 15 | Meanness vs. Drama vs. Bullying

GOAL:

To get students to clarify the differences between thoughtless, mean and bullying behaviors

MATERIALS: SITUATION CARDS (4-6 sets)

ACTIVITY: Divide students into groups of 3- 5 students. Have students work with their group to decide whether the action would be categorized as bullying, mean, normal conflict or harmless behavior.

DISCUSSION: As a whole group, discuss each card. See if there was agreement about how to categorize the behavior. Allow students to discuss and debate.

Have students discuss definition of:

- Online Bullying Behavior
- Online Mean Behavior
- Online Normal Conflict Or Misunderstanding

Part of the challenge with meanness, drama, and thoughtlessness is that the rules and expectations are still evolving about: 1) who is allowed to share information and 2) how they do so.

HANDOUT:

Situation Cards

Make 4-6 copies of this page so that each student group has a full set. Cut out each situation and glue to an index cards (one situation per card). Each card describes an unfortunate or challenging situation, feel free to add other situations that are relevant to your group.

Tasha makes plans with a friend to meet after school. The friend doesn't show up and sends a text that reads "can't come."	Joe shares a picture of someone where it looks like he is picking his nose. The caption says "picker."
When Steve plays video games online he gets overly competitive and usually ends up putting his opponents down, getting sarcastic and using all caps. He acts in ways he would never act at school or in a sports game.	Two friends are mad at each other. One friend posts about her friend's secret knowing her friends would be hurt and embarrassed.
Kim's friends spent an hour last night in a group chat. Kim was not included. When she asked about it, her friends told her they did not notice.	Kim's friends spent an hour last night in a group chat. Kim was not included. Danielle had wanted to include Kim but Eloise told her not to invite her.
Lane takes a picture of a classmate's selfie (Tom) and writes, "Tom takes the dumbest pictures of himself." 4 classmates "like" the comment. Friends of Tom post that Lane's comment is mean and he should take it down. Lane posts, "stop making drama, lol."	Lauren forwarded an email Steve wrote without Steve's permission. Steve had not wanted anyone else to see what he had written.
Lane takes a picture of a classmate's selfie (Tom) and writes, "Tom takes the dumbest pictures of himself". 4 classmates "like" the comment. Friends of Tom post that Lane's comment is mean and he should take it down. Lane takes down the picture.	Every night Bill posts something anonymously about his classmate on AskFM.
You are playing and winning an online game. Your opponent is a friend of yours and keeps calling you a "jerk." Eventually, he quits and goes offline. He won't respond to your invitations to play.	Shawna shares a picture on Instagram from her birthday party. Not all her followers were invited to the party.
Your best friend posts a picture of herself and another friend. The caption says, "BFF."	Two friends are mad at each other. One friend posts about her plans for the weekend. The other friend comments, "lame."
Reese was chosen MVP of the team. She was excited to tell everyone at school the next day. Gaby's sister was at the game, told her and posted the news.	Dan posts his friend's low score on the big test in Math.

LESSON 16

Preventing Cyberbullying: Using the Screen to be Mean

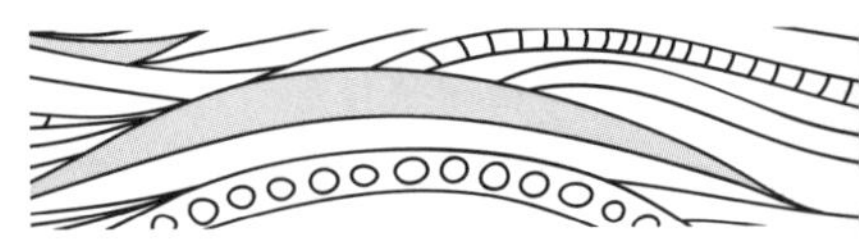

GOALS:

- To be able to discern what is funny and what is mean
- To think about the impact of your online activity on others
- To understand the definition and impact of cyberbullying and what actions may be considered cyberbullying
- To learn how to deal with a cyber bullying situation and understand the importance of seeking help from a trusted adult

MATERIALS: HANDOUT 16.1, Funny or Cyberbullying HANDOUT 16.2, Using Screen to Be Mean Scenarios

BRAINSTORM: Have students brainstorm responses to the questions below. Write responses on large paper or white board. Examples are provided but have students generate their own responses.

What are some of the ways that you and your friends tease each other online for fun?

- Send jokes back and forth
- Alter photos of one another, in a goofy (not mean) way

How do you know when teasing "crosses the line" and becomes harmful? What are some signs, and what does it feel like to be in that situation?

- The teasing is not funny anymore.
- You feel helpless, powerless, feel like crying, or wonder "Why is this happening to me?"
- You feel embarrassed, feel worried about what others think of you, or concerned about your reputation.
- You are thinking about the teasing a lot and dread seeing the teaser.
- You are worried about your safety.

How are people mean on screen?

- Sending a mean email or IM to someone
- Posting mean things about someone on a website
- Making fun of someone in an online chat
- Doing mean things to someone's character/ creation in an online world
- Pretending to be someone else
- Spreading rumors
- Forwarding embarrassing photos
- Posting/ emailing/ texting cruel comments
- Purposely excluding someone

What is cyberbullying? What types of behavior/actions would be considered cyberbullying?

Cyberbullying is the use of electronic communication to bully a person, typically by sending messages of an intimidating or threatening nature. Cyberbullies usually bully repeatedly, with the intention of causing hurt feelings.

ACTIVITY: Funny or Cyberbullying?

Show students examples of text provided messages on HANDOUT 16.1 one at a time. Ask students to decide if the text was fun, good-natured joking around or cyberbullying? Ask students to think if they were a parent or teacher reading the text, would they think it was good-natured joking or cyberbullying?

GROUP DISCUSSION:

How does the person being bullied feel?

Hurt, humiliated, powerless, small, sad, angry, invisible

What is the difference between being bullied in person vs. being bullied online?

- Information online can spread rapidly and reach more people quickly.
- Being bullied online can be very public.
- You can be bullied online all times of day.

Why would someone be mean online?

- Seek power, status and attention

ACTIVITY: On HANDOUT 16.2 are some common situations where people say mean things online. Discuss the first situation as a whole group. Then divide the students into groups of 4 and give each group a situation. Put the following questions on the board and have each group answer the questions about their scenario:

- Was there mean behavior?
- Why do you think the person behaved that way?
- How did the target feel?
- Is this cyberbullying?
- What can the target do?

Whole Group Example:

Evan plays on a website where he can build a fortress. One day Evan goes to the site and finds his fortress has been destroyed. At school, everyone seems to know that his fortress was destroyed and everyone is laughing. Evan is upset and confused. Later that night, he rebuilds his fortress. The next day, it is destroyed again.

What do you think happened?

How do you think this made Evan feel?

- Is someone destroying his fortress on purpose?
- Is it happening more than once?
- Is this cyberbullying?
- What should Evan do?

DISCUSSION:

When someone is mean to you online, you have choices:

- Ignore
- Block the person doing the bullying behavior
- Get off digital device or site
- Don't let them know their efforts worked
- If mean online continues, you need to tell a trusted adult

Cyberbullying is the use of electronic communication to bully a person, typically by sending messages of an intimidating or threatening nature. Cyberbullies usually bully repeatedly, with the intention of causing hurt feelings.

HANDOUT 16.1:

Funny or Cyberbullying?

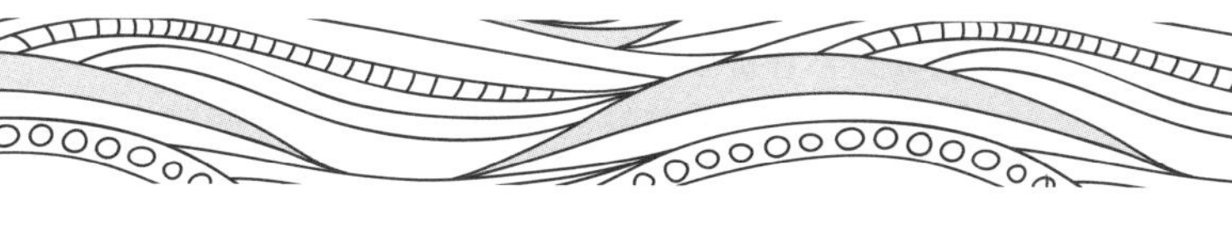

When Thomas gets here, no one talk to him!

Did you hear about Tania?

You stink, LOL!

Did you see what Kelly wore today? HA! Can you say disgusting?

I'd rather die than have to be partners with him.

He's so gay.

Hate you, JK

Get a life!

Don't invite her. She would ruin the party.

Where did you get that shirt? Babies R Us? JK

HANDOUT: 16.2

"Being Mean on Screen" Situations

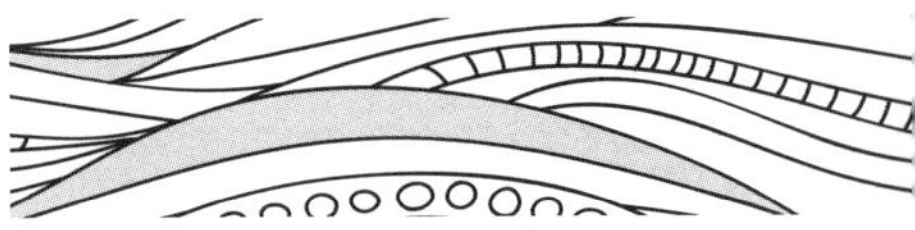

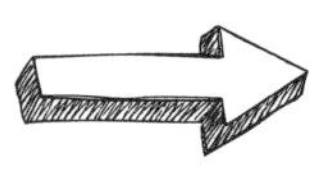

Kelly is in a chat room with her friends. She knows everyone in the chat room. One day someone entered that they did not know and started asking what grade they were in and where they went to school.

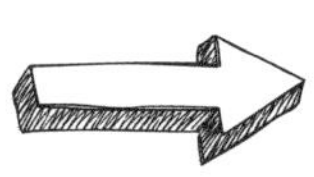

Alanna keeps getting text messages from someone saying means things about her. The person sending the messages doesn't use a real name, but Alanna can tell the messages are coming from someone who also makes fun of her at school.

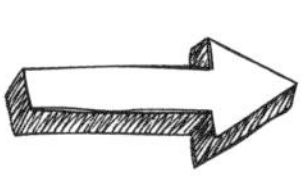

Jessica is a new girl at school and she is making a lot of friends. A classmate created an anonymous email account info@ihatejessica.com. She then posted manipulated pictures of Jessica. Jessica doesn't know about the account but another classmate does.

In an online game, students can be in one camp. All of Brad's friends were in his camp and having fun together. One of brad's friends, Neil, who moved away last year, joined the online game for the first time. He created his own camp and all of Brad's friends left his camp and joined Neil's camp. When Brad was online the next day, he was shocked and hurt to find his friends had left his camp. In anger, he typed "You jerks." All of his friends got mad at him and did not talk to him for a few days.

Sophia was invited to the amusement park by her friend, Amy, from school. Sophia had already committed to go shopping and to the movies with her neighborhood friend, Ava; this outing is to celebrate her birthday. Sophia really wanted to go to the amusement park with Amy. Amy is taking a bunch of people and she did not want to miss out. Sophia ended up lying to Ava, telling her she was sick, and she went to the amusement park with Amy and her friends. Sophia had a great time and felt good about her decision. While she was having fun at the amusement park she posted a picture of herself and the group of friends, saying, "Having fun at Six Flags." She posted it without thinking.

Shelly has a crush on Jake. Diane knows Shelly likes Jake but she likes him too. Diane keeps taking snapshots of herself and Jake hanging out and sends them to Shelly. Diane hopes to make Shelly jealous so she will either back off and let her have Jake or do something that makes her look silly.

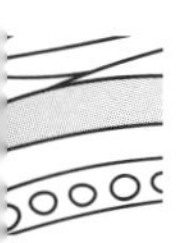

LESSON 17 | The Ups and Downs of Anonymity

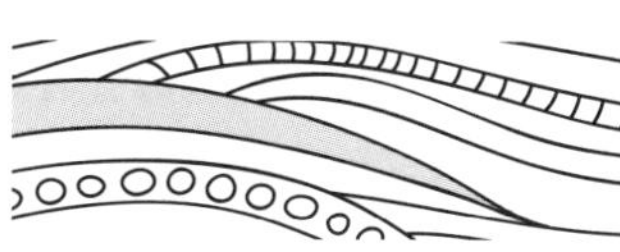

- To help students to understand that anonymity changes human behavior, often for the worse.
- To promote thinking through the impact of anonymous communication, understanding it is not just a prank.

MATERIALS: Masking tape, taped across the floor in a long line

Two signs, one saying "AGREE" and one saying "DISAGREE"

Both HANDOUT 17.1 and HANDOUT 17.2

ACTIVITY: Ask students what it means to be anonymous.

Read the statement below, ask all of the students to stand somewhere on the piece of tape that reflects the degree to which they agree with the statement. Then ask each student to reflect on why they chose where they are on the continuum.

Agree ....Disagree

Statement: "People act mean and hostile toward each other when they communicate anonymously."

BRAINSTORM: Split the group into two groups. Read the statement below:

Statement: "If you were creating a website for kids to talk to each other/socialize online would you want it to be anonymous"

Have one group identify the PROs of anonymity. Have the other group identify the CONs of anonymity. Each group should come with at least 5 Pros or Cons.

DISCUSSION: Have students complete HANDOUT 17.1 anonymously. Then discuss each question as a group.

ACTIVITY: What Would You Do?

Divide class into 6 small groups (or 3 groups would get 2 scenarios). Give each group a "What Would You Do" Scenario from HANDOUT 17.2. Give groups time to decide how to handle each situation and then have each group present and share with the whole group.

HANDOUT: 17.1

The Impact of Anonymity Worksheet

> What forums are out there for people to post anonymously?

> Why do they exist?

> Have you been on a site where kids post anonymously about other people?

> Have you ever posted something anonymously?

> Has anyone ever shown you something someone wrote about you anonymously?

> What are your choices if someone posts anonymously about you?

> Why do people post anonymously? Do you ever know who is posting? How do you know?

> Why wouldn't someone be willing to share their thoughts and stand by them?

> Do kids need places to be able to share anonymously?

> In what kind of situations?

> Why do we care what unidentified people think of us?

> Can you think of times where people are generous or kind anonymously?

HANDOUT: 17.2

What Would You Do?

SCENARIOS

> What would you do if...
Someone shows you a forum question asking which girls are nasty, and your name is on the list?

____

____

> What would you do if...
Someone shows you a forum question saying your best friend is rude and talks too much?

____

____

> What would you do if...
Someone says your best friend is gay? You already know this--he's your best friend. But not many people know this yet. People are being mean to him.

____

____

> What would you do if...
Someone posts that you were with your best friend's boyfriend? It is true but it was impulsive and harmless.

____

____

> What would you do if...
Someone anonymously makes a hot list? Everyone is adding to it.

____

____

> What would you do if...
A mean comment is posted anonymously about one of your teachers and many classmates "like" it?

____

____

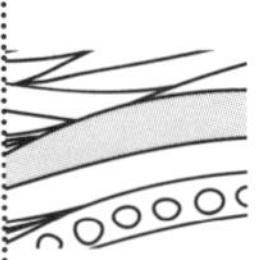

LESSON 18 | To Tell or Not to Tell

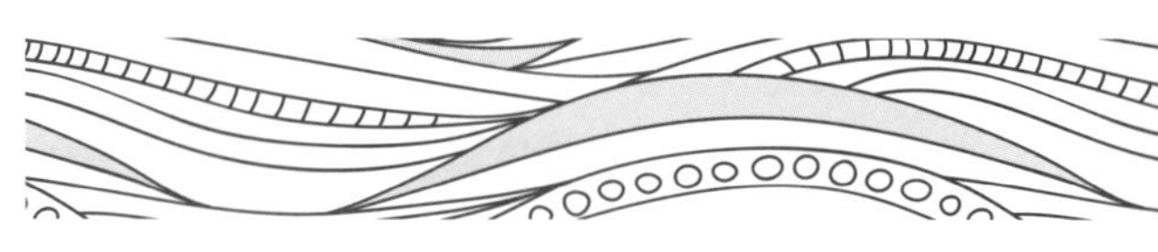

GOALS:

- To help students understand the importance of telling when there is trouble.
- To help kids discern when to tell and facilitate discussion of student's fears about telling on a peer or classmate.
- To help youth realize that others would also tell an adult if they were in the same situation and that adults want to know.

MATERIALS: Situation cards, HANDOUT "Tell or Not Tell" Situation Cards

ACTIVITY: Back to Back

If space is available, have students sit on the floor in a big circle. Two students will come into the middle of the circle and sit back to back. Students will take turns being in the middle. The teacher will read a situation card from the handout. The students in the middle of the circle will each need to decide if, given the information, they would tell an adult (teacher, parent, coach, family member, etc). If they would tell, the student gives a thumbs up. If they would not tell, the student would give a thumbs down. Once each student in the middle has decided they turn and show each other and the class. Each student explains their choice. Then, ask all the other students to show thumbs up (for telling) and thumbs down (for not telling). Ask students to provide information on how they came to that decision. Encourage discussion. Once students have spoken, highlight the difference of opinion and under what circumstances telling is warranted. After the students have spoken, the leader can provide guidance.

DISCUSSION: When should you tell an adult about online behavior?

Anonymity in online spaces is a complex concept. It is especially important to teach young people how to navigate these dynamics in order to be empowered to stand up—or to seek help from a trusted adult—when they encounter mean-spirited, hurtful behavior.

HANDOUT: 17.2

"Tell or Not Tell" Situation Cards

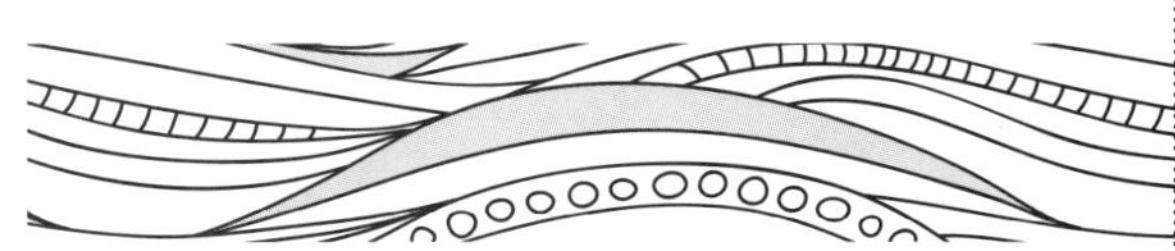

Your friend sends you a text with a swear word.	You overhear that a classmate is posting things about you on a social networking site, apparently it has happened more than once.
Your friend sends a text with a rumor about another friend.	You were reading a classmate's blog and he was writing or implying that he was depressed and wanted to hurt himself.
All your friends get in a group chat each night and don't include you.	You saw a picture of a friend of yours posted with a comment that said "ugly."
A friend got a pocket knife for his birthday, posted a picture of it and said he would show everyone at school tomorrow.	Your classmate posts a racist comment.
Friends are in a group text with you plotting a prank on a classmate.	You are sent a picture of a person at your school. In the picture the person is wearing inappropriate clothing.
You keep getting insulting texts from an unknown number.	Your friend checks her phone and starts to cry.

TOPIC 6:

Moving Forward: Wrapping Up

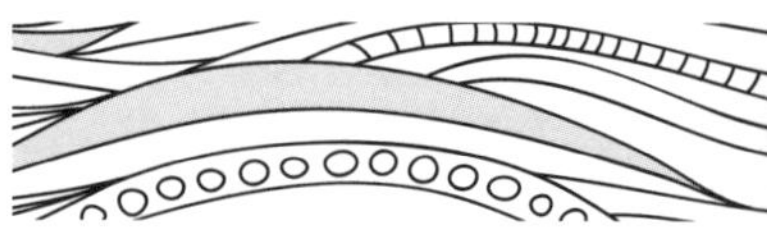

Giving students a chance to do some peer teaching around thoughtful digital engagement is a great way for them to incorporate, demonstrate and own their knowledge. These final exercises offer students a chance to do just that. These exercises leave students feeling empowered in their digital interactions. The unplugged challenge is a great bonding experience and will also help students critically observe their own powerful relationships with digital devices. By raising awareness these exercises help students focus on what is positive in their connected lives and notice things they may wish to change.

Lessons include:

Lesson 19:
Pass It On: Leading Younger Digital Citizens

Lesson 20:
The Unplugged Challenge

Lesson 21:
The Power of Digital Kindness and Positive Change

LESSON 19 | Pass It On: Leading Younger Digital Citizens

GOALS:

- To have students explore these common challenges in the digital world
- To empower students to be a positive role model online and to others

MATERIALS: A recording device

BRAINSTORM: Ask students to brainstorm "awkward moments" with digital technology. Examples include:

That awkward moment when your mom reads your texts.

That awkward moment when you see your younger sister's sexy selfie.

That awkward moment when your teacher takes your phone because you were using it in class and your texts are way too embarrassing.

That awkward moment when your friend group texted and told the world you had a crush on someone.

ACTIVITY: Have students create a project that teaches how to be a responsible digital citizen.

PROCEDURES: In this exercise students will dramatize a challenge that they have experienced with social media and then they will share their videos with classmates or a group of younger students and facilitate a discussion. Creating a video is a great way for students to dissect the social dynamics that they experience. Teaching with self-created material deepens their knowledge and empowers them. This exercise will help students sharpen their skills and confidence.

1. Make a list with the whole group of problems/issues that have come up this year related to digital communication. Ask students to recall situations they or a friend saw or experienced and/or issues that you would want younger kids to be aware. Each issue becomes a possibility for a video lesson.
2. Have students choose scenarios they would like to work on. Students can rank their top three scenarios.
3. Match the groups (3-5 students per group) using their preferences and your own prior knowledge of social dynamics.

4. Students design and produce a short video. Video should portray a problem, the impact or potential impact of the problem on various people, and show appropriate resolution of the issue. For preparation have each group think about:

Describe the problem. What happens?

What's the setting?

Who are the people?

How do each of the players feel?

Does anyone need to calm down?

What are the possible solutions?

Which solution is chosen, why?

Does the solution work?

If it did not work, choose a different solution.

5. Have students present their videos to younger students.

DISCUSSION: How do these videos help the younger generation?

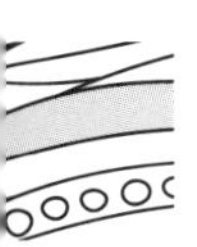

LESSON 20 | The Unplugged Challenge

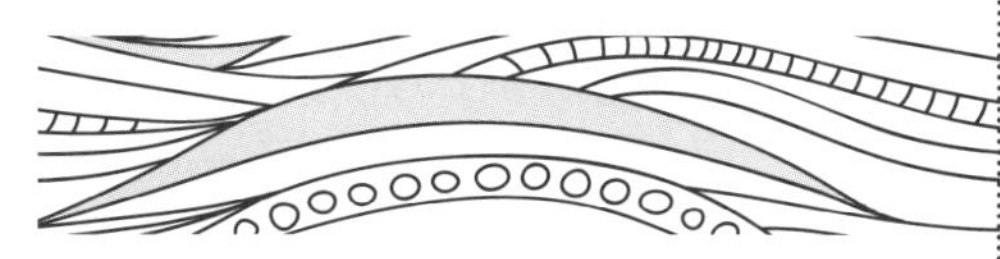

GOALS:

To have students experience a respite from some of the stresses of a connected life, which offers a perspective on which digital activities are affirming and which may be draining. The leader/teacher will gain more solidarity if he or she also attempts a digital sabbath or "fast."

MATERIALS: HANDOUT: Daily Diary for Unplugged Exercise

If you are at a camp or youth group, you can collect everyone's phones and chargers. Otherwise, this is up to them.

ACTIVITY: Choose an evening, a weekend or another set period of time in which you and your students can unplug. Have them keep a paper journal of their unplugged experiences. You may want to run this as a voluntary activity or even a fundraiser. Are there parents or others in the community that will pay per unplugged hour or day?

Have the students keep notes in their journal of what times in the day they feel most discomfort at not being able to check in with texts or social media. Or do they feel relieved?

In conjunction with this challenge, you may want parents in your school community to arrange a time at home when the family "unplugs" from electronics.

BRAINSTORM: In advance, brainstorm through student resistance. When they say it is "impossible" to unplug, have the class come up with solutions.

DISCUSSION: Go around in a circle and have each student say the best and worst thing about being unplugged as a conversation starter. Then identify a few common areas to discuss. Closing questions: Would you unplug again? Why or why not? Would a regular unplugged time every week be a good idea? Why or Why not?

For Further Reading: In preparation for this exercise, the Leader may wish to read: *The Winter of Our Disconnect: How Three Totally Wired Teenagers (and a Mother Who Slept with Her iPhone) Pulled the Plug on Their Technology and Lived to Tell the Tale* by Susan Maushart. If this exercise includes parents, you may wish to suggest this book to parents in your school community as well.

HANDOUT:

Daily Diary for Unplugged Exercise

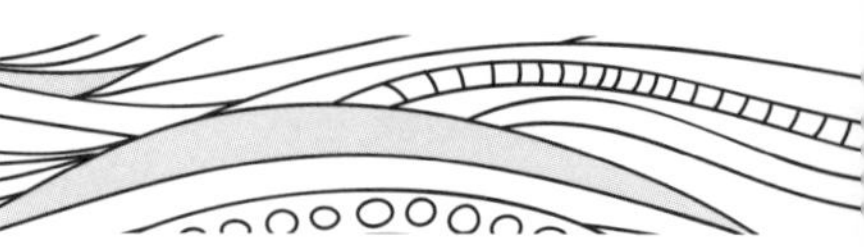

{Morning}

I connected with my friends by ____.

I felt like looking at my phone or computer ________________________________ times.

I really missed ____.

It was kind of a relief not to have ____.

{Lunchtime}

I communicated with others by ____.

I felt like looking at my phone or computer __________ times.

I really missed ____.

It was kind of a relief not to have ____.

Check in # 1: Write 2-3 paragraphs on a separate sheet about your experience so far.

{Afternoon}

I felt like looking at my phone or computer ________________________________ times.

I really missed ____.

It was kind of a relief not to have ____.

{Evening}

I spent more time ____.

I felt like looking at my phone or computer ________________________________ times.

I really missed ____.

It was kind of a relief not to have ____.

Check in # 2 Before bed: Write 2-3 paragraphs on a separate sheet about your experience.

LESSON 21

The Power of Digital Kindness and Positive Change

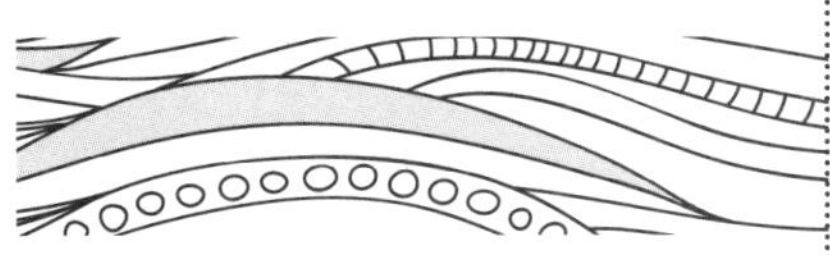

- To help students realize the positive impact of digital technology
- To encourage students to notice the power of online communication to make a positive difference in the lives of others and notice acts of kindness that occur every day
- To promote mindfulness and a sense of digital citizenship

MATERIALS: Access to digital device with internet connection either during the session or later at home

ACTIVITY: Set aside time for students to search the internet for examples of kindness or positive impact.

Examples: The Ice Bucket Challenge where people dared their friends and family to be filmed having a bucket of ice water poured on their heads or donate money to the ALS Association went viral on social media during the summer of 2014. The campaign has raised $15.6 million in a few months compared with $1.8 million raised in the same time period last year.

Facebook initiative increased the daily number of people who register to become organ donors by 21-fold on a single day last year, according to a recent study in the *American Journal of Transplantation*. That finding is hopeful news for the 100,000-plus Americans who are currently on an organ-transplant waitlist. It's also an indication of the powerful impact social media can have on public-health campaigns.

Give a Random Stranger a Gift – Find a public wish list online and send a gift to a stranger.

Share a positive blog post – When you turn on a television, open a newspaper, or check your e-mail, chances are you'll hear negative news of some sort. It's easy to let all the negative news in the world bring us down. So strive to be a source of positive information for others by going out of your way to share fun or inspirational blog posts or online articles with your friends and family.

CHALLENGE: Set up a challenge for your group, grade or school that encourages use of digital media in a way that fosters random acts of kindness or involves everyone in an effort that has a positive impact. Have group brainstorm various ideas and vote on the idea that is most feasible and easy to implement. Brainstorm goal of project and tasks involved in creating this project; create a timeline. Have students sign up for tasks. At conclusion of project have students write about their experience.

Definition of Terms

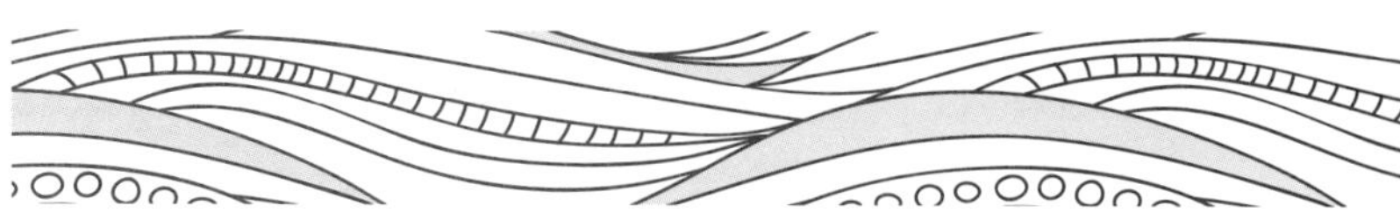

Applications and websites that some of your students may be using.

Instagram: Instagram is a photo and video sharing app that allows users to take pictures and videos, apply a digital filter, and then share them online with followers. Users can also post their Instagram photos on Facebook, Twitter, Tumblr, and Flickr with the option of adding a location tag. Reminder: When you create your account, all Instagram photos are posted publicly unless you change a setting (meaning anyone can see them). Your students may wish to go in to settings and make their photos private. Watch out for young people measuring: "success" of their photos – even their self-worth – by the number of likes or comments they receive. Ideally, it is better that kids don't try to validate their popularity or crowdsource their identity this way. You can find disturbing pictures of self-harm, violence, pornography, and drug use on Instagram, so even if a teen's profile is private they can see content that may be inappropriate.

(Instagram is rated 12+ and has a 13+ age requirement.)

Facebook: Popular with adults and some teens, this is currently the largest social network, with over one billion users worldwide. Some young people have been abandoning Facebook because their parents are using it, but many young people still have an account. Facebook can link to other applications as well.

Vine: Vine is like Instagram, except with video. Some people call this kind of video sharing "micro-vlogging." Vine allows its more than 13 million users to share video clips of up to six seconds. The app, which is now available on iOS and Android devices, is used by news reporters, comedians and Twitter users that have more than just a picture to share.

Keek is like Vine – it is a video sharing app. The videos on Keek can be slightly longer, but otherwise Keek is very similar to Vine.

Snapchat: Snapchat is an app that allows users to share photos, videos, and messages (or "snaps") with a list of contacts. Snapchat users can set a time limit for how long recipients can view their snaps (from 1 to 10 seconds). After the specified time range ends, the snap disappears from the recipient's device. As your students will point out to you, the recipient can take a screenshot of the snap, saving it for as long as they like. Or they can take a picture with another camera. So, like all shared images, video or text, once you share, it isn't in your control anymore. You can also text in the app, and send video in real time, so parents may be looking at their children's texts but not see texts that are sent in an app like snapchat.

(Snapchat is rated 12+ and has a 13+ age requirement.)

Note: For users under 13, Snapchat offers a similar service called SnapKidz.

Definition of Terms

Kik: Kik is a smartphone messaging app that allows users to send text, pictures, videos, sketches, and more all within the Kik app. Unlike some other messaging apps that are based on a user's mobile number, Kik identifies its users with unique usernames. Kik allows for easy group texting. Like Snapchat, Kik offers a space to text that parents may be less aware of. (Kik is rated 17+ and has a 13+ age requirement.)

Yik Yak: Yik Yak is an anonymous messaging app that uses GPS location data to display the most recent posts by other Yik Yak users around you. It allows for people to interact with others within a certain geographical boundary without having to know them. Many schools disallowed Yik Yak after some schools were closed due to threats posted on the app. Unlike many apps, you can see things posted in Yik Yak without registering for your own account. (Yik Yak has a 17+ age requirement.)

Whisper: Whisper is an app that lets users anonymously share messages. The app works by having its users type what they want to share (called "whispers") into the app, and then attempts to match it with a stock image based on the content of that message. Users can also use their own images. While Whisper is anonymous, users can still comment on or "like" other whispers, as well as send private messages. Many people post very sexual or disturbing "whispers." (Whisper is rated 17+.)

Secret: Similar to Whisper, Secret is an app that lets users anonymously share messages (or "secrets") with others. What differentiates Secret from Whisper is that the secrets users share are done so with members from their social networks, instead of with strangers. However, Secret does not tell you which of your friends is also using the app. No user names or profiles are needed for "secrets." (Secret is rated 12+ and has a 13+ age requirement.)

Tumblr: Tumblr functions as a searchable platform for "microblogs" or a cross between blog and Twitter: Like a constantly updating scrapbook of photos, text and/or videos and audio clips. Users create and follow "tumblelogs," or short blogs that (if posted publicly) can be seen by anyone. So while they may feel like a diary, they are NOT private. Many young people have personal Tumblrs to share content like photos, videos, random thoughts, and other things they find funny with their friends. This online hangout can be creative and artistic but sometimes also explicit. Like on Instagram or Twitter, graphically sexual images and videos, depictions of violence, self-harm, drug use, and offensive language are easily searchable.

Privacy can be protected, but this is not the default. If a Tumblr user wants a private profile it has to be a second profile, which can be protected by password.

It is easy for content to be reblogged and shared in a different context. Many young people and Tumblr users want their content reblogged and shared.

Definition of Terms

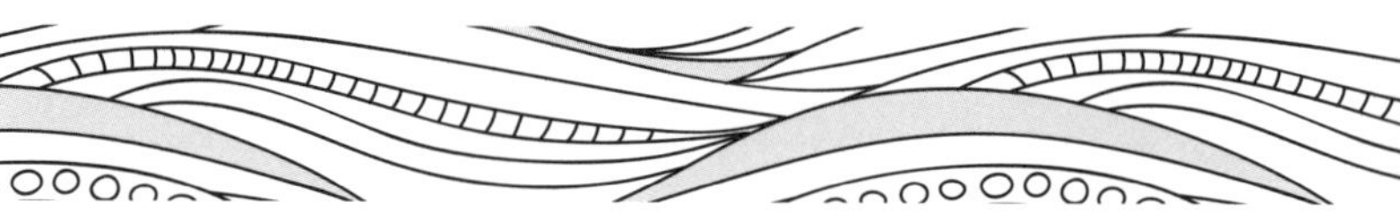

Twitter: Twitter is a microblogging site that allows users to post brief, 140-character messages – called "tweets"– and follow other users' activities. Some young people like it because it is a quick way to share updates with friends. It's also handy for keeping up with the latest: breaking news, celebrity gossip, etc. Posts appear immediately and even if you delete, someone could have seen and shared. Tweets have gotten athletes, students and politicians in big trouble! Also, your child can follow celebrities on Twitter, but they are basically getting marketed to by a professional social media account holder.

Ask.fm – Ask.fm is a social website that lets kids ask questions and answer those posted by other users – frequently anonymously. Because most of the traffic here is anonymous, there are numerous unkind comments and explicit sexual comments. This site is a place where kids can go to ask questions about what people "really" think of them and their peers (or sometimes strangers) can comment anonymously – often leading to cruelty.

You can turn off anonymous answers but for many users the social aggression and explicit comments are part of the attraction of using the site.

Top Games:

Minecraft: Very popular, open ended game. There are unmoderated forums for players so your students can be playing with strangers. Very simple, non frightening graphics. Collaboration is an important part of the game, but conflicts can arise in the game that can affect friendships.

Clash of Clans: Very popular strategic game, players are supposed to be 13 and up. Some violence but not graphic. There are in-app purchases.

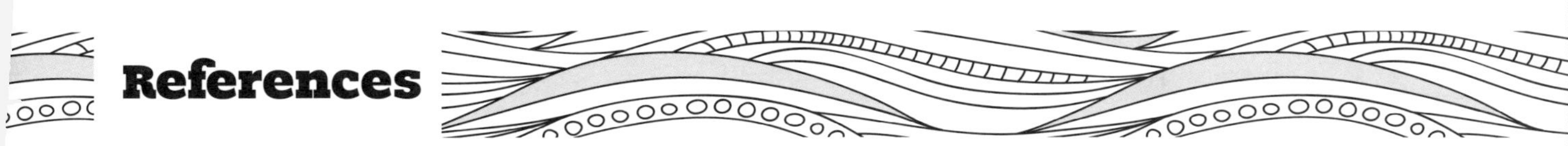

References

Teens, kindness and cruelty on social network sites (Pew Research Centers Internet American Life Project RSS) http://www.pewinternet.org/2011/11/09/teens-kindness-and-cruelty-on-social-network-sites

About the Authors

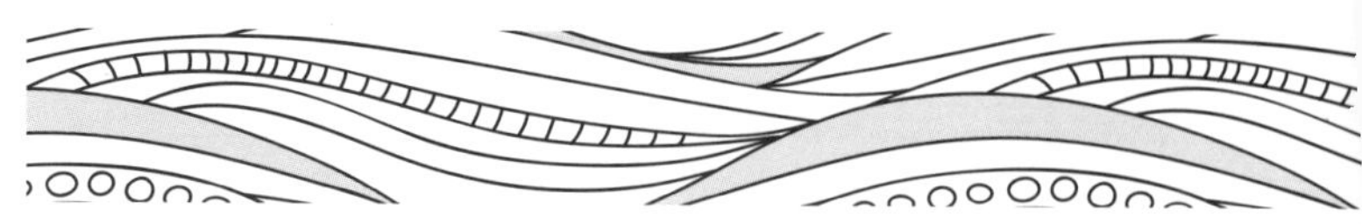

Devorah Heitner, PhD

Founder: Raising Digital Natives

Dr. Devorah Heitner has been helping people have important conversations about technology, communicating with empathy and social media for the past ten years, first as a professor of media studies and now as the founder of Raising Digital Natives (www.raisingdigitalnatives.com), a resource for parents and schools seeking advice on how to help children thrive in a world of digital connectedness. An experienced speaker, workshop leader, and consultant, Dr. Heitner serves as a professional development resource for schools, consulting on responsible digital citizenship, digital policies, and parent engagement. She enjoys working with excellent public and independent schools across the United States, offering parent talks, student workshops, and trainings for faculty and administrators. Dr. Heitner has spoken at numerous conferences including the Family Online Safety Institute Conference, the National Association of Independent Schools Conference, and many others. She is currently writing a handbook for parents, "Raising Your Digital Native."

Dr. Heitner has a Ph.D. in Media/Technology and Society from Northwestern University and has taught at DePaul University, Street Level Youth Media, and Northwestern University. She is delighted to be raising her own digital native, too. You can contact Dr. Heitner at devorah@raisingdigitalnatives.com.

Karen Jacobson, MA, LCPC, LMFT

School Counselor, Family Therapist and Parent Coach

Karen has worked with children and families for over 20 years. She received her Master's degree in Counseling Psychology from Northwestern University and extensive training from The Family Institute at Northwestern University. In addition to private practice, Karen has over 10 years of experience as a school counselor helping children, pre-teens and teens develop skills, face challenges, own their voice and power and ultimately know, love and accept themselves. She has worked in both private and Chicago inner city schools and has expertise in challenging behavior, school difficulties, peer/friendship issues, bullying, self-esteem, teen pregnancy and school violence. As a co-founder of Parenting Perspectives, Ms. Jacobson works with parents by teaching effective parenting strategies that enable them to enhance their connection with their children and create peaceful, loving homes. She has developed and presented over 25 different workshops to thousands of parents and teachers. Her highly acclaimed course, Becoming a Conscious Parent: Tools and Principles for Parenting from Your Heart, based on their Ten Principles of Conscious Parenting, enhances parent's self-awareness, broadens their parenting choices, strengthens the parent-child connection and fosters resilience, responsibility, and self-esteem in their children. Karen has been a keynote speaker on many topics including, Raising Respectful, Responsible and Resilient Children in a Privileged World. Karen joyfully parents her two teenage boys. You can contact Karen Jacobson at karen@parentingperspectives.com.